THE
TICKET
FULL
DISCLOSURE

NOT-SO-SPECIAL
SPECIAL EDITION

THE **TICKET**
FULL DISCLOSURE

The Completely True Story of the Marconi-Winning Little Ticket

a.k.a., The Station That Got Your Mom to Say "Stay Hard"

FOREWORD BY DARYL "RAZOR" REAUGH

SCOTT BOYTER

BENBELLA

BENBELLA BOOKS, INC.
Dallas, Texas

BENBELLA

BenBella Books, Inc.
6440 N. Central Expressway, Suite 503
Dallas, TX 75206
www.benbellabooks.com
Send feedback to feedback@benbellabooks.com

Printed in the United States of America
10 9 8 7 6 5 4 3 2 1

Library of Congress Cataloging-in-Publication Data is available for this title.

ISBN 978-1933771-68-7

Proofreading by Jennifer Canzoneri
Cover design by Laura Watkins
Illustrations by Ralph Voltz
Text design and composition by John Reinhardt Book Design
Printed by Bang Printing

Distributed by Perseus Distribution
perseusdistribution.com

To place orders through Perseus Distribution:
Tel: 800-343-4499
Fax: 800-351-5073
E-mail: orderentry@perseusbooks.com

Significant discounts for bulk sales are available.
Please contact Glenn Yeffeth at glenn@benbellabooks.com or (214) 750-3628.

CONTENTS

SECTION FOUR
BaD Radio

SECTION FIVE
The Hardline

SECTION SIX
Where Are They Now?

SECTION SEVEN
In for the Long Haul

Mind Vitamins

Daryl "Razor" Reaugh
Dallas Stars broadcast analyst

W HEN I WAS APPROACHED to write the foreword for this book, my initial thought was one of confusion.

Why was a guy with a twelfth-grade education (a Canadian one at that) and no working knowledge of what a "forward" (sans stick and skates) actually is, being courted to provide a literary *hors d'oeuvre*?

The answer to that just might be as old as The Ticket itself—a statement that doesn't really mean anything, I just thought it sounded profound and was a tie-in of some sort.

I arrived on the Metroplex sports scene while the Little Ticket was still in its embryonic stage. Ticketchicks were a little sweeter and a whole lot cleaner. Norm was the competition. And Byron Nelson had a sense of humor—halcyon days for sure.

Fast forward fifteen years and the Ticketchicks are tart and dirty. Norm is the enemy within. And Nelson is trying to be "about the golf." All of which (watch your necks here) brings me to Line Four Guy.

To me, Line Four Guy personifies The Ticket—all smarmy and smart while at the same time intrusive and addictive. But he is also what every P1 aspires to be—he's on the channel, he's part of the show and he's managed to breach the wall (or the screener, in this case).

Over the years we've come to know much of who The Ticket's on-air "talent" really are. Craig Miller is a biker and paints clowns. George Dunham raises a household full of boys, yet still finds time to pursue a passion for all things botanical. Bob Sturm hunts neighborhood cats for both sport and profit. Corby Davidson is a shoe model who lives and breathes Oklahoma football. Rhyner bows at the altar of the American pastime, and also likes baseball a lot. The stable is full, and it's packed with verbose, clever testosterone-ies. But we know very little about who this Line Four Guy is.

Some rumors have circulated as to his background, one of which had him growing up in a family of eleven children in Wink, Texas, where as a kid he was kicked in the head by a mule. The person who relayed this story to me said he met the entire family and came to the conclusion that the mule must have been very busy.

Another unsubstantiated peek into Line Four Guy's world suggested that he was a mechanic by trade. They said he was either a damn good mechanic or a really bad one, that it was just hard to tell by the forty or so vehicles littering his front yard.

One of his siblings was said to have gone into law enforcement, which made Line Four Guy's family very proud. But she was asked to leave the force when she refused to arrest the community's biggest dope dealer—her husband, Nathaniel "Powder" Rochet, who specialized in distributing "The Devil's Dandruff."

Razor channels his inner and outer Herb Brooks for a good cause: Team Musers and The Ticket's Charity Challenge on Ice.

One thing is for sure: he, like many others at The Ticket, is a world class whiskey drinker. Time of day is said to mean nothing to Line Four Guy; neither do the seasons, the geography nor the social situation.

Perhaps that's part of his genius.

And genius really is what The Ticket puts forth.

From a guy who calls in to Line Four every afternoon, to Fake Jerrys and Fake Tigers. It's the intelligent sports debate and the frivolous current event discussions. The yuk monkeys and the ticker updates. The Ticketchicks and the marketing/sales babes.

It's a format that has tried to be copied both locally and elsewhere—with frigid to tepid results at best.

So why is it that this works on 1310 while struggling at other stops on the dial? I think it succeeds because The Ticket is a perfect amalgamation of personalities with the marketplace. The legion of Ticketheads and P1s that has swelled over the past decade and a half are as brand-loyal as a Winnebago full of NASCAR fans, and those casual listeners (the ones who don't listen to The Ticket but say they find Gordo's Corner to be both "appointment listening" and "eargasmic") stop by for their guilty pleasure more often than they want to admit. And when they do, Sportsradio 1310 The Ticket gives them, and all others who get with the channel, exactly what they Q-tipped their earholes for.

If you flipped past this foreword in order to get to the actual meat of the book you purchased (as I usually do), then *touché* brotha! But if you took the time to read it, and you connected with the energy and the love that I tried to transfuse into the preceding paragraphs— then, well, I'll remember to leave the seat down.

SECTION ONE

From the Back of the Bus to On the Air

1

RHYNER'S DREAM

THE STORY OF HOW Mike Rhyner, Craig Miller, George Dunham and Greg Williams evolved from press box yuk monkeys to forming the core of one of the nation's most popular radio stations—one that features masters of the art of "guy talk"—should be fairly well known.

What may come as a surprise is the fact that if Rhyner's wife hadn't been bored one Sunday, there's an excellent chance The Ticket would never have existed.

On a random Cowboys Sunday in 1990, Renee Rhyner (who, by the way, coined the name "The Ticket") took her two-year-old daughter Jordan to the park. She met a lady, started talking with her, and found out that the lady's daughter and Jordan attended the same daycare. They saw each other periodically in the park over the next few weeks, and as their conversations increased, they came to find out both of their husbands were in the radio business.

Before long, the Rhyners were invited to the house of Renee's new friend. Her husband, Geoff Dunbar, would be the lynchpin in what would eventually become The Ticket.

"Geoff Dunbar is the forgotten man in all of this," Mike Rhyner said. "We started talking about our days in radio—who we knew, who we didn't, and all of that. I went over there and talked with him; we weren't big buddies or anything like that, but we talked quite a bit.

"We talked about why there was no all-sports radio station in Dallas," Rhyner said. "Would it work? What would it take to make it work? Every time we got together, the conversation would get back to it. It would dominate the conversation, in fact."

The operative thinking in Dallas was that a sports-radio station wouldn't fly because of WBAP. They were just too big. They had a powerful signal, one that reached to Chicago when the weather was right. They had the Mavericks. They had the Rangers. They had the untouchable Randy Galloway. You just couldn't compete with them.

"That made no sense to me," Rhyner said. "Anybody can be competed with. Anyway, as we kept talking about it, I realized I must have been giving this more thought than I realized, because I had a lot of things fairly clearly mapped out. It just kind of went on and on with [Dunbar] like that for a couple of years."

Time to take a shot

At the time, Rhyner was transitioning from a job with GTE On Call, a service that provided sports updates to callers for a few cents per minute. This was back before the Internet took control of the world, so a service like that was actually viable. He had left GTE to take a job doing sports with KZPS-FM (92.5). It was OK, but Rhyner was in his forties, and he hadn't really taken a shot at snagging the big fish, so to speak.

That was about to change, and in a hurry, when Dunbar called him one day in June of 1993.

"Geoff called and said, 'Let's go have lunch. I found a guy who wants to play radio,'" Rhyner said. "We stayed about three hours.

All the time I'm talking and he's writing everything down. He wanted me to replay every discussion we'd ever had. That was the first time anything tangible that would later turn into The Ticket happened."

"Originally it was more nuts-and-bolts-type stuff we talked about," Dunbar said. "You had Norm Hitzges on KLIF. How were you going to go up against him? Who was available, and were they any good? There was a lot of talk of concept, but the concept wouldn't work without a frequency.

"We didn't really talk about 'OK, we're going to have this guy in the morning and these guys in the afternoon' or anything like that," Dunbar added. "But once we decided it would work, we had to figure out who to talk to. Who was tanking in the market and would take the risk and change format.

"I looked at all the frequencies to see if any owners had the foresight to take that risk," Dunbar said. "Nobody really did until we made our move on 1310."

Rhyner and Dunbar agreed that Rhyner would use his contacts to recruit on-air talent, and Dunbar would use his to get a money guy. Rhyner didn't have to look real far to find his guys. In fact, he knew who they were all along.

Fun and yuks

Through Rhyner's work for KZEW-FM (97.9, better known as The Zoo), GTE and KZPS, he had gotten to know Greg Williams (who was working at WBAP) and Craig Miller (who was at KRLD) through the times they'd shared in various press boxes throughout the Metroplex. While they were laughing it up in what was normally a reserved place of work—pissing off a lot of reporters and writers in the process—Rhyner realized the three had formed a unique connection that could pay off someday.

"I met Greg first," Rhyner said, "and he knew more about me than I did about him. But the minute he started talking, I knew I

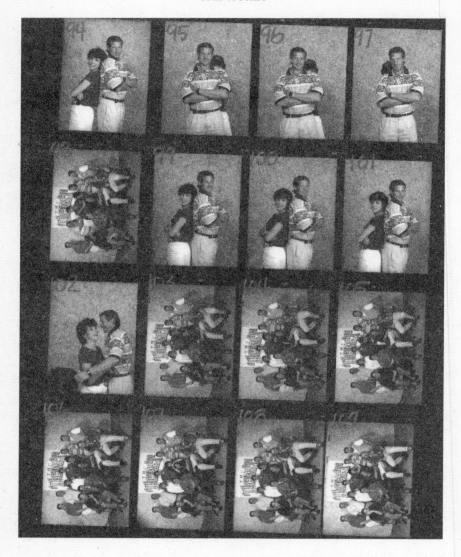

liked him. Then Craig started showing up, and the three of us became recognized as a clique. You hardly ever saw one of us without the other two in tow."

"I always listened to Mike when he was on The Zoo, and I thought he had the absolute best job in the world," Williams said. "He got to be around rock 'n' roll music and got to go to games. I thought,

'My God, it doesn't get any better than that; you're on the best radio show in the Metroplex, you get to cover games and you get to cover athletes.'

"The first time I met him was in the auxiliary press box at old Arlington Stadium. I was totally intimidated by him," he said. "I didn't recognize him at first, but when I went, 'Who's that?' and somebody told me who he was, I was terrified. I wasn't even that terrified when I interviewed Magic Johnson."

Later they did start talking, and Williams amused Rhyner. Williams compared the auxiliary press box environment to a prison. They had the "real writers," the real important people, in the press box behind home plate. Then way out in right field was "the back of the bus," where all the spares sat. Williams was the sparest of the spare, along with Rhyner, David Robinson, Craig Miller and writers from the University of North Texas paper who would cover games.

"You know how in a prison you've got inmates who kind of run it?" Williams said. "Me, Rhynes and Craig Miller kind of ran the back of the bus. We were always the subject of conversation. We had our own seats and nobody else ever dared sit in them.

"Both of the press boxes were so bad it was pitiful, but to get in the door to the auxiliary box you had to literally walk across the roof. It was a very minor-league setup. We did get free food, though. You don't ever bitch about free food."

Williams, Miller and Rhyner were inseparable. They covered every Rangers home game, helping each other out while constantly trying to crack each other up. Williams said he'd get behind Nolan Ryan when Miller or Rhyner were interviewing him and make faces.

Ask any of the three about specific press box conversations and answers are hard to come by—after all, this was nearly twenty years ago. But Williams did bring up a nugget of a different sort.

"There was this one time I remember," Williams said. "We were on the third level, so it was a pretty long drop. We'd always open the windows up—if we wanted to. If we didn't want them open, they were closed.

"They gave out these pens shaped like baseball bats," he said. "I was fucking around with one, and I dropped it. It was like a missile. Junior gave me that Junior look, and Rhyner just said, 'Greggo.' Boy, I just took both hands—I was sitting in the middle—and just pretty much moved back and said, 'Don't anybody look out that window. *Nobody*.'

"Junior and Rhynes were giving me the business the whole time; they were cracking up," Williams said. "But I was horrified; if that had hit somebody in the head, it would have impaled them! But nothing came of it."

Near the end of the game, the "bus riders" would head down near the field to watch, and then head through the dugout to the clubhouse for post-game interviews. That required, obviously, a little bit of time sitting amongst the paying crowd. Williams sometimes had a bit of a problem turning off the profanity he was so accustomed to using in the press box. When there were obvious signs Williams was about to launch into a tirade containing multiple "F-bombs" and the like, Miller issued a PVS warning—Potentially Volatile Situation.

"There was one particular conversation I remember, and it took place at old Arlington Stadium," said Miller. "Near the end of each Rangers game we would leave the auxiliary press box [and go] down to the stands, where we'd sit for the last inning. After the final out we'd go through the gates right by the first-base dugout. From there we'd go to the clubhouse.

"Anyway, one time it was me, Rhynes and Greggo, and we were behind home plate," Miller said. "There was a family of four sitting right in front of us. Greggo started talking, and I remember turning to Rhyner and saying, 'This is a PVS.' Right after I said that, Greggo starts cussing it up. 'That fuckin' Juan Gonzalez...' Meanwhile, the dad's looking back at Greg and the mom's covering up the kids' ears."

Although he's suffered some embarrassment at times, Williams said he never had any actual confrontations with fans over his raw vocabulary. "If that had happened, I would have diffused it; I would

have profusely apologized," Williams said. "I was used to being in the press box, and I couldn't adjust to being in the stands. It got to the point where Rhyner would sit a couple of rows in front of me and act like he'd never met me—it was a little pre-Ticket distancing.

"But it was a blast up there," he said. "It was a constant state of laughter."

The trio talked about baseball, their jobs, anything and everything. They were loud, they were laughing, they were cutting up—generally acting the way you're not supposed to act in a press box.

But then Rhyner began to notice how everybody else was reacting to them. There were those who seemed to be listening and wanted to get in on it, and others who absolutely hated it.

"It didn't matter whether it was a Cowboys, Rangers or Mavericks game," Rhyner said. "It was odd and interesting that these guys were reacting to it the way they did, but I didn't think much of it until later, when I realized there was something useful in play here.

"When Geoff told me he had a guy interested in making this happen, I was thinking how to get Greggo and Junior in on it," he said. "This was what all those nights at the ballpark, all the cutting up in the press box, was leading to.

"I was the equals sign in this crazy equation: on one side I had a guy who wanted to play radio and another guy who knew how to do it, while on the other I had some talented guys I knew I wanted to be a part of it. The hardware was on one side, the software on the other. My job was to get them together."

They eventually did get together, of course, but not before a wild, gut-churning ride filled with uncertainty, anger, alleged inaction and downright bitterness.

2

THE ROLLERCOASTER

A S RHYNER WORKED to build the team that would form the core of The Ticket, Geoff Dunbar had found somebody who "wanted to play radio": investment banker Spence Kendrick. But as the proposed December 1, 1993 launch date for the station drew nearer, uncertainty gave way to uneasiness, then to downright queasiness, as everyone involved wondered if this dream would ever become reality.

"There were days where in the morning the whole idea was scuttled, then in the afternoon it was back on," Rhyner said. "The next day it was the same thing. It was a real seesaw."

Rhyner had the dual problems of worrying that his vision would not achieve fruition and allaying the fears of the people he was bringing on board—Greg Williams, Craig Miller and George Dunham. All of them had quit their jobs in anticipation of The Ticket becoming a reality. Rhyner had also convinced already-established radio personality Skip Bayless, who had in turn recruited Chuck Cooperstein to get on board.

"It was real tough for me because I was the guy they were calling, saying, 'Hey man, what's going on here?'" Rhyner said. "I had to do a tap dance to assuage them, telling them this was going to happen, while knowing I might damn well be lying to them.

"There were things going on behind the scenes that today they still don't know about," he said. "I couldn't tell them that stuff; if I had it would have shaken the foundation. There are some things in this world you're better off not knowing. If I had told any of the guys what was going on, they could have gone back to their jobs pretty easily. Their former bosses had patted them on the head and said, 'OK, run on out there to play. When you see the folly of this, we'll take you back.'"

Things were shaky on the financial side, to say the least.

Dunbar said he was introduced to Kendrick through a mutual friend—an investment banker himself—who had worked with Kendrick in New York. Another friend of Dunbar's was married to Kendrick's cousin. Kendrick said it was Dunbar's father Chuck who introduced the two—the first of many differences in Kendrick's and Dunbar's versions of how things went down back in the day, as will soon become apparent.

One thing isn't in question, and that's the fact that they first met in the spring of 1993.

"I said, 'Here's what it will take money-wise,'" Dunbar said. "'Can you put it together? Don't worry about anything else; just find the money.'"

Dunbar had been down this road before, trying to get a radio station off the ground. He had helped launch stations before and knew it would take about $3–5 million just to buy the frequency. It would have to be on the AM side of the dial, because even a floundering FM station's frequency—with a crappy signal—would run a minimum of $6–10 million. That's just the cost of doing business in a Top 10 radio market.

Kendrick, meanwhile, had always had a fondness for radio, going back to childhood, when he went to sleep with a transistor radio under his pillow. And he'd grown up listening to The Zoo, so he knew Rhyner. Kendrick said the first time he met Rhyner, he "beat him down with about a thousand questions" about Rhyner's time at the station.

"We decided to try to fit everything together," Kendrick said. "The original idea was that I was going to raise the money, be the business side of it. Geoff would do the sales side and Mike would be the talent guy."

The original plan called for Kendrick and his investors to purchase frequencies in both Dallas and Houston, which just happened to be the two largest U.S. media markets without all-sports radio stations. While places like Sacramento, San Bernardino, Hartford and Norfolk had the format, the two largest cities in Texas were doing without. It sounded like a slam-dunk idea; however, the Houston plan was quickly scrapped.

"We started talking about negotiating for both, but the Houston transmitter site was in the middle of the tollway that loops the city," Kendrick said. "You were going to have to move the tower, so it would become more of a real estate deal than a radio deal. We dropped that and focused on 1310."

And that focus shifted to selling some rich guys on the idea.

"I told Spence he'd probably get a lot of tire-kickers, guys who [only] say they can do things," Dunbar said. "He didn't blink at the dollar figure, but he didn't know anything about the radio business. I told him that $3 million would be the cheapest he could get into it. And that was just to get into the game—that didn't include actually operating the thing.

"When you ask people for money who say they can do it, I've found you have to pressure them enough to see if they're actually committed," he said. "Once people get to a certain threshold of money to put up, it becomes apparent pretty quickly that they're either going to lose it or get it done. That's the point we had to get Spence to."

Dunbar said Kendrick told him he was going to leave his investment banking position within thirty days to pursue financing The Ticket full time. Over the next few weeks Dunbar would occasionally check in with Kendrick to see how he was progressing.

Suffice it to say, Dunbar was disappointed with what he heard.

"The first thirty days he hadn't done anything," Dunbar said. "I think it was more of a game to him, because he'd become enamored with WFAN when he was living in New York. He'd never even seen the inside of a radio station. He didn't know what it would take and didn't realize we would be going up against forty other radio stations in one of the most competitive markets in the country."

Kendrick wasn't sitting completely still, though. By July he had submitted an offer to Bonneville Broadcasting for the 1310 AM frequency, putting up a non-refundable deposit of $200,000 out of his own pocket.

However, notice the term "non-refundable." The deadline to pay the remaining part of the balance, $2.8 million, was approaching. The deal was $3 million: $2 million in cash, and the rest Bonneville would take in the form of a note due the following April.

And then the deadline passed. Bonneville agreed to extend it, but Dunbar was in full panic mode.

All in

It was December 15, 1993. The station had already missed its originally planned air date, and the staff was getting restless. Dunbar alleges that Kendrick refused to pay anybody, even though they had quit their jobs up to a month and a half before on the promise they'd be getting paid by the beginning of December.

"These guys needed to be paid whether or not we were on the air," Dunbar said. "We're talking ten days before Christmas. But Spence didn't want to cut a check to anybody. He said he wasn't going to pay anybody until we went on the air, and that may not have been for another ninety days. I went nuts. I told him, 'Spence, everybody left their jobs. You agreed to pay them.'

"I told him, 'You're going to be dead. These people are going to cook you. You'll have no standing, no validity whatsoever,'" he continued. "The friend of mine who was married to [Spence's] cousin went up to him and said, 'Listen, you little shit. This is the way it is. Just because you don't want to pay them doesn't mean they should suffer. *You* suffer.'"

But Kendrick was able to produce two checks, both dated December 1, which were written to George Dunham and Chuck Cooperstein. He also showed several other checks he had written to members of the sales staff, and other checks that had gone toward operating costs. Kendrick had successfully persuaded a few investors to come on board, but most of the expenses were coming out of his own pocket.

Still, there was definitely Trouble in River City as of early January 1994. All the people involved with the station were starting to look like idiots around town because the station's launch had been announced a month before. Everybody in Dallas radio was laughing at the buffoons behind this so-called "Ticket" because nothing was happening. Norm Hitzges was reportedly predicting it would be at least another six to nine months—if ever—before The Ticket would sign on.

"Not ever having been in the business, Spence's timetable wasn't what it should have been," Dunbar said. "We didn't have any money. He was thinking we'd be OK if we would have gone on the air by April 1. But the Cowboys were going to be in the Super Bowl. If we didn't get on the air before that game we'd be toast for a year. We'd miss millions of dollars in revenue; we'd lose everything."

In a last-ditch effort to force the guy who "wanted to play radio" into realizing the seriousness of the situation, Dunbar brought Bayless in to meet with Kendrick. He said Kendrick was elated to have Bayless on board, but Bayless wasn't that elated himself. In fact, he was pissed that he hadn't received assurances of a sign-on date, much less a paycheck.

And the Super Bowl was only two weeks away.

"The first thing Spence wanted to do when he met Skip was to get Bayless to sign a copy of a book he had written about the Cowboys," Dunbar said. "I thought, 'What the fuck? This ain't a jock-sniffing thing here.' But that's kind of where his head was. He was already rich; he didn't have to worry about making a dollar. It was becoming real apparent he wasn't going to be able to close the deal.

"Anyway, we had a 'come to Jesus' meeting and we used Bayless," he said. "He, Rhyner and I were in cahoots. Mike and I had already talked to Spence and told him—in no uncertain terms—that we had all these people on the air side and the sales side who were getting impatient, to say the least.

"We had a meeting and Bayless told him, 'I'm out of here if you don't show me the cash,'" Dunbar said. "We brought him in because he was the guy Spence was enamored with, and now the guy whose jock strap he wanted to sniff was going to walk. Not only was he going to walk, Bonneville was going to walk with the money. We finally got Spence to realize the seriousness of what was happening."

Kendrick really didn't have much to say about the details of the meeting, although he did admit it served the purpose of showing him how important it was to get the station on the air before the Super Bowl. "By the end of it, I said we'd be up and running," Kendrick said. "Skip Bayless grabbed a piece of paper and wrote, 'We will be on the air January 24th, 1994' and I signed it."

However, he adamantly denied Dunbar's implication that he was some trust-fund baby who didn't have his nuts on the line just like everybody else. "I worked for everything I had, and I was putting up a substantial portion of my net worth," Kendrick said. "When I paid these guys when we weren't on the air, I didn't pay myself. I was in a position where I had to get something done. There was a tremendous sense of urgency.

"As far as the idea that I wasn't willing to pay them goes, well, the proof's in the checks."

Second thoughts?

Bayless may have been the one to speak up, but everybody else was uneasy too. Especially Rhyner, who was not only in limbo, but in the position of trying to keep everybody from jumping ship.

"I went to bed many times thinking the next day the thing was going to go under, and miraculously enough it never did," Rhyner said. "But I was working more on what I thought than what I knew.

"I didn't have a lot of control over what was happening; I'd hear one thing, get a certain feeling about it, then tell [Williams, Miller, Dunham, et al] something else," he said. "I had to put on a brave face for them. Meanwhile, a lot of the time I talked to Spence I walked out of there thinking, 'God, this is going to go under before it even gets off the ground.'

"Spence was putting on a brave face for me, but I got the feeling what he was telling me wasn't what was really going on."

Remember, this was Rhyner's big shot at the big time, probably the only one he would get. So as he saw his dream slipping away, he had to face the bitter realization that maybe he'd have to start all over.

"I was going to see this through until there was nothing to see through anymore," Rhyner said. "If the worst had happened—and I don't know how I would have done this, because I was the last guy in the world to try and do something like this—I would have picked it up myself and gone to anyone I could have gone to and tried to get them interested in it.

"Who would I have gone to? I knew there was this guy named Mark Cuban out there, and I could have told him about it even though I didn't know him at the time," he said. "But I'm sure anybody I would have talked to would have seen right through me and known what a piker they were dealing with. They'd probably say, 'Here's a chance to screw this know-nothing to the ground.'"

Miller also had his doubts, and was worried he might have to find a new career.

"I don't remember my friends or family wondering if anything was wrong or anything like that," Miller said. "Everybody was supportive. They figured I knew what I was doing and what Rhyner and everybody else was doing.

"There's no way I would have gone back to my old job at KRLD," he said. "I remember when I gave my notice to the program director, he said something to the effect of, 'When it doesn't work out for you, you're well-liked here. You can always come back and we'll make room for you.' But I don't think I ever would have done that. I think I would have turned the page and tried to find a job somewhere else."

"I wasn't concerned about it at all," Williams said. "Rhyner was brilliant at keeping all that stuff away from us. It never occurred to me they were having money problems. When I heard the stories after we were on the air, it gave me the willies.

"I had enough money saved up that I could make it," he said. "It was going to be December 1 [that we went on air], then December 15, then January 1, but I was able to get by. A couple of weeks later they called us into Baker's Ribs on Greenville and told us we were going live on January 24, whether or not the Cowboys were in the Super Bowl.

"It wasn't a feeling of relief when I heard it, it was just happiness."

Kendrick also kept the faith, and his confidence, even while all those around him feared their dream would fade into oblivion. "It never came to the point where I thought it wouldn't happen," Kendrick said. "There was a lot of concern from the talent standpoint, obviously. They were all friends, and when one of them got nervous there was ripple effect. I saw it at times, but I saw it less than anybody else.

"But I had confidence in myself and I believed in the idea," he said. "I was staking a lot of money, and once you go hard on something like that, it's tough to walk away. Once everything started falling into place I felt pretty good about it. Despite all the ups and downs, I knew it was going to get on."

Kendrick was surprised at the how difficult it was to convince investors to get on board to fund what seemed like a no-brainer. He said he approached more than a hundred people to pony up but met with a lot of resistance for several reasons.

"All the facts were there for this idea to be a slam-dunk, but there is no such thing," Kendrick said. "It doesn't matter whether you're talking about fifteen years ago or today—people always ask questions. The investors I was talking to, some of them I knew from New York and they trusted me. They said if I was involved they'd get involved. Other guys had to be sold on it.

"These were guys I was asking to invest $50,000 to $250,000 a pop; they don't get to that position without asking good questions and being pretty savvy on the investment side."

One of the main problems was that most of the on-air talent—with the exceptions of Bayless, Cooperstein and, to some extent, Rhyner—were basically unknown quantities. The other was that the station didn't have the rights to any of the local sports teams' broadcasts.

"These guys were third or fourth team at other stations," Kendrick said. "The challenge was to get the investors to understand that the talent we had was really good; they just hadn't had the chance to show it yet because they were behind guys like Randy Galloway and Brad Sham.

"The investors either liked or didn't like Bayless, but they knew him," he said. "And they knew controversy was good. They liked that the format was successful in other markets, but the fact that we didn't have a team as an anchor created a lot of resistance. The conventional thought was a sports station could only be successful with a team. But WIP in Philadelphia had proven otherwise through creativity."

The White Knight

Bayless, when he wasn't fuming about the lack of follow-through in terms of getting the station on the air, was writing a *Cowboys Insider* newsletter that was faxed to subscribers—the kind of thing you could make a pretty good chunk of change doing before the Internet was in just about every household.

The backer of the newsletter was David Vaughn, the man who would eventually be credited with saving the deal. Bayless introduced him to Kendrick, and he soon expressed an interest in making it happen. Without subjecting everyone to the tiredhead created by spelling out the numbers involved, suffice it to say that Vaughn's investor group came through with enough money to satisfy Bonneville and get the station up and running by the self-imposed January 24 drop-dead date.

Finally, the station was going to be a reality. But if you think all was right with the world, think again.

No hard feelings? Yeah, right.

Dallas radio icon Ron Chapman told Dunbar that The Ticket's launch was the greatest ever in this market. All three major television affiliates were there to cover the station's first day, helping to generate an enormous, immediate buzz. The Ticket got more coverage in its first ten minutes than most stations garner in five years.

But The Ticket was operating on a shoestring, and a frayed one at that. Sharing a cramped studio with KZPS (much more on this later) created hard feelings, as did the lack of equipment that all the on-air staff had been accustomed to at other stations.

"This is how fucking stupid this was," Dunbar said. "We had to rent a studio and had no phone system, no nothing. I'd been involved with stations in towns of three thousand people that had been better operated than this.

"We sent everybody to the Super Bowl in Atlanta, but because we didn't have any money I had to get the cheapest flights and the cheapest hotels," he said. "And all that time we were trying to act like we were a big-time operation."

"I'm operating out of rented studios with one board, a production room I've got to share and no office space for the sales staff," Dunbar added. "I can't hire enough sales people because there aren't any benefits.

"It was like a monkey fucking a football."

Dunbar's sales staff was able to soldier on, despite having to share a single computer. They were closing deals left and right because advertisers were foaming at the mouth to be a part of this sensation. It also didn't hurt that The Ticket had the cheapest ad rates in town.

"But we still didn't have what we needed, not by a long shot, and everybody was getting pissed," Dunbar said. "They'd come to me saying, 'Geoff where are our benefits? Where's this, this and this? This is bullshit.'

"I'd tell them I didn't write the checks, that they'd have to ask Spence," he said. "And he was pissed off, like I was trying to undermine him. I'd have knock-down drag-outs with him. I said, 'Spence, this is the job you wanted. You wanted to be GM, you have to answer the questions. You have a lot of people's lives and families depending upon you doing what you said you were going to do. And when you don't, they get pissed off and come to me.'"

Another source of friction, Dunbar said, concerned who was getting the credit for the station's launch. Dunbar said Kendrick was mad because Dunbar was getting the face time. "The TV stations wanted to interview me because I had put it together, plus I knew most of the guys doing the interviewing," Dunbar said. "There was no ego involved; they just knew me. But Spence was livid; he wasn't getting any ink and it was his toy."

Kendrick didn't want to get into a lot of "he said, she said" arguments regarding Dunbar's assertions. But he insisted on presenting his side on certain topics, and this was one of them.

"If you talk to anybody who was involved with it, it was never about me. It wasn't my 'toy'; it was an investment for me that became a passion," Kendrick said. "It was my first deal I did by myself. After everything that happened, and after we sold it, investors did spectacularly."

Obviously, it wouldn't be long before Dunbar and Kendrick parted ways. It came one Friday morning when Kendrick told Dunbar he was fired.

"I knew it was coming for a while, but I was still pissed," Dunbar said. "I almost came over my desk and threw him out a tenth floor window. I said, 'You can't even spell "radio" and you're going to run this?' He was going to bring in some cronies of his who knew nothing about what was going on.

"I was pissed off for a long time, but I never bad-mouthed the station," he said. "It would have been like kicking your own child. Spence helped those guys make a fortune, but I ended up with a firm grip on the shit end of the stick."

It would be easy to dismiss Dunbar as a bitter old man, but that would be a mistake. He's gotten over his bitterness, and today teaches high school in Colorado while trying to put together a renewable energy company.

Add to that the fact that a few years ago he was able to beat what was termed terminal cancer by his doctors, and Dunbar is able to keep his Ticket days in perspective.

"It was timing predicated on really smart, educated guesses, and we pulled it off," he said. "All the pieces just happened to fall right into place."

To say the station experienced growing pains, however, would be a vast understatement.

3

PUTTING IT TOGETHER

THE TICKET was finally on the air, but at the time, that and 25 cents would get you a *Dallas Morning News*. The station was sharing a studio with KZPS in Addison, and the guys were feeling like interlopers, second-class citizens and redheaded stepchildren, to put it mildly. To say the studio's setup was Spartan would be giving short shrift as well. They may as well have been working out of the back of a van down by the river.

And the on-air talent—with the exception of Skip Bayless and Chuck Cooperstein, and to a lesser extent Mike Rhyner—was an amalgam of no-names with zero recognition among the masses; these were guys who, for the most part, had received their shot because they liked to shoot the shit with Rhyner in Dallas-area press boxes.

"What was it about those guys that made me want to bring them on board?" Rhyner said. "They were smart, they were funny and they entertained me. I thought to myself, 'These are guys I'd like to listen to. If I were the average, spare guy out there listening to this, I'd dig it.'

"The difficult thing for me was to bring this side of the equation and the other together and make it all work."

Taking a chance

Rhyner had a small amount of equity in the company, but he still had to convince Spence Kendrick and Geoff Dunbar to take a chance on a bunch of guys nobody had ever heard of. And their anonymity nearly drove Rhyner to abandon his involvement in The Ticket altogether.

"I tell you, it was not easy," Rhyner said. "I had to really talk the powers that be into letting me bring these guys nobody knew aboard and giving them a chance. That didn't get rubber-stamped. I remember the blank looks on [the investors'] faces when I would mention their names.

"I would like to think I did a decent job of convincing them that these guys would be able to make a go of this thing and make it successful, even if nobody knew who they were," he said. "A far more practical reason was I really didn't think we could have paid anybody who was a big name. Norm wasn't in the mix—anybody who was big back then was not a player for me. I couldn't go get Randy Galloway, I couldn't get anybody. We weren't that well financed. And maybe that turned out for the best, in hindsight."

Whether for practical reasons or merely because of the gut instinct he had that his press-box buddies could make it work on big-market, big-time sports radio, Rhyner was convinced they would be a success. And he was willing to stake his entire dream on bringing in "his guys."

"I just told [the investors] 'Look, I know these guys have something, and we can do what needs to be done here. I really believe in them; these are the guys I want,'" Rhyner said. "I said, 'If you don't go along with me on this, I'm probably not the right guy for what you're trying to do. You told me to go out and recruit talent, and I did that.'

Coop, Rhyner and Skip at one of the first remotes.

"I had told myself that I was going to do this the way I wanted to do it," he said. "If they had told me I couldn't have the guys I wanted, I would have walked away and never looked back. At any time, if the resistance had become too untoward, I was always prepared to walk away. This never became a long-term thing for me until pretty well down the road."

But no matter how funny or engaging Williams and the rest of the guys were, it was crystal clear that if this thing was going to be a success, they were going to have to set themselves apart. Straight-up Xs and Os would doom The Ticket to failure, and Rhyner knew it.

"I told all of (his fellow hosts) we had to be different, but I don't think they ever really wrapped their arms around that," he said. "We were all kind of slaves to the way things had always been done, and they thought successful sports talk was successful for a certain reason, and that those were the things we needed to embrace.

"They were very, very leery when I would talk to them about that kind of thing."

"What attracted me to The Ticket wasn't something that had to do with content as much as the concept of an all-sports station," said George Dunham. "I had heard about the idea, and thought it would be great to be at a place where sports generated everything you were talking about. You didn't have to worry about how much time sports was getting because it wouldn't be up against news or music.

"I had thought to myself for a while that if I could be at an all-sports station, that would make my life a lot easier—it would be utopia," Dunham said.

Home sweet home? Not exactly.

So the team was put together and they were off and running. Well, maybe "off and at a slow jog" would be a more accurate way to put it. While everyone was ecstatic to finally be on the air, that feeling soon gave way to frustration over the conditions under which they had to work.

The Ticket rented their studio space in Addison, sharing it with the much-more established FM station KZPS. KZPS staffers considered these new sports guys to be nothing more than an inconvenience, and station management went so far as to assign a person to "watch" The Ticket guys to make sure they stayed in their space, so to speak. They weren't supposed to use anything they didn't own; they couldn't even use the KZPS typewriter.

"It was ridiculous," Dunham said. "The space we had wasn't built to do a talk show. We couldn't see the Ticket ticker guys because they were down the hallway. Plus, the KZPS people were really annoyed with us."

The space The Ticket hosts used to broadcast was set up for an FM station and wasn't at all conducive to sports talk. To be effective in that format, the hosts have to be in close proximity to the board operator and the producer, who, when the hosts are taking callers, can quickly tell them who's dialing in.

Elf and some guy named Mike with Michael Moroney: the first Ticket promotions director and inventor of Ticketstock and "The Two-Minute Drill."

That wasn't the case there. The producer had to sit in another room down the hall where he would answer the phone. He'd get the call, write the name on a piece of paper and sprint to the studio and give the paper to the host.

It was minor league, and it was a pain in the ass for everybody concerned.

It was one of the strangest, most bizarre arrangements anybody had ever seen. This was before deregulation really took hold in radio, before companies could own six, seven or eight stations in the same market. Back then, a company could own only two stations in a given market; one AM and one FM. It would only make sense, then, that two stations housed in the same office would be owned by the same company.

But nothing made sense about this situation.

"You had two radio stations owned by two different broadcast entities sharing space, essentially," Rhyner said. "It was very, very weird. KZPS assigned a guy who I had worked with at The Zoo, John Michaels, to watch us and make sure we didn't steal anything.

The 1998 Ticketstock at Plano Center.

I think the world of John; I just love that guy. But at the time he was kind of the gendarme up there.

"No question about it, we were the biggest bastard children you could imagine," Rhyner continued. "All the ZPS people looked at us funny. And I'd known a lot of them for years. They'd see me, shake their head and go, 'What the hell are you doing? Who told you that *you*, of all people, could do something like this?'

"A lot of them had been in the business for years before I got into it. They looked at me like I was their junior partner or something."

Rhyner said that, years later, he took the high road whenever he ran into his former "roommates," long after The Ticket had become a huge success. "I never got in their face; I have too much regard for those people to ever take that approach with them. Those people have been very successful in their own right, and most of them are glad this worked out for me the way it did. Most of them are impressed by what we've done; they've told me that, and that means a lot to me. It means a lot to get some level of approval from them."

That's sweet, and should damn near give you a warm fuzzy just reading it. But the fact remains that the KZPS guys weren't too sweet to anybody from The Ticket back in the day.

"It was lousy and we were second class," Miller said. "You had the established FM station and they all kind of looked down on us like we were interlopers. But for a while we didn't care because we were on the air and we were happy. Then it became a beating. It was awful.

"At least we knew it was temporary."

"We were in a studio that wasn't set up to do a talk show," Williams said. "The microphones weren't synced up. It was awful. If we dropped a pen or a piece of paper, you heard it.

"Plus, they were a bunch of pricks," he continued. "They wouldn't let us do anything. I was on the phone one time and one of them told me, 'You can't use that phone. You have to use this one.'"

It did get a little bit better after a few weeks, but it was clear The Ticket had to find its own space.

"It had to happen; there were just no two ways about it," Rhyner said. "We couldn't go on like that. As time went on, John Michaels began to soften up a little bit. He began to see what was going on over here and saw that we were having a little fun. He became very intrigued by it all. He began to turn his head to certain things, you know, [like] using the ZPS phone and typewriter.

"Still, we needed to get the hell out."

After three irritating months they finally did, to an old studio on Mockingbird Lane in Dallas that had been owned by KLIF. "It was a feeling of elation once we had our own home, but as happy as we were, I guarantee you that the ZPS people were happier we were gone," Rhyner said.

"We felt like now we had a little bit of certainty. It took a little of the tenuous nature out of things," he said. "By no means were we out of the woods, but by that time I was past the point of worrying too much about the day-to-day of it. I wasn't worrying about the station meeting payroll, things like that.

"Other people were still probably feeling some trepidation," Rhyner added. "But we always managed to somehow stay afloat.

Maybe that means things weren't as bad as I thought they were. I'm one of those worst-case-scenario guys anyway. That's just how I roll. Sometimes I tend to magnify things a little bit."

Leaving the KZPS space was more than a simple move to another office. It created a feeling of legitimacy around the station.

"It was like we were a real radio station," Miller said. "We had our own cubicles; we had a conference room where we could have show meetings."

"That's when I think The Ticket really started taking off, when we started taking on the air some of the funny conversations we had off the air," Dunham said. "That's where The Ticket culture really got started. Before, we were kind of like guests in someone else's home; we didn't really know what to do."

Taking it to the people

The change in scenery was undoubtedly a huge factor in The Ticket becoming so successful so quickly. But a lot of that rise was due to repeatedly taking the shows and personalities on the road. A car audio place one day, a liquor store the next, a car dealership after that. It was all part of the master plan to take The Ticket to the people, making the personalities part of the fabric of the Metroplex.

All of that sounds great. But the strategy was really born out of necessity because the station still didn't have the budget to advertise itself. This grassroots approach had to be taken in order for the station to become financially viable. However, the strategy paid off, not only financially, but also by giving listeners a chance to put faces with the hosts' voices, and giving the hosts the chance to learn firsthand what "Joe from Balch Springs" liked and what he hated.

And all that one-on-one interaction forged a bond between the talent and listeners that lasts to this day.

"Once the station was on the air, revenues began to climb," said Dunbar. "But we still didn't have a promotions budget. It was crazy;

The first Guys' Night Out: Coop, Greggo, David Burrall, Rhyner, Craig, Steve Pryor, George, Mark Elfenbine, "Ticket Ted" Gangi and Bill Jones.

we had nothing.

"So how do you get as much bang for the buck without spending anything? You send everybody out on remotes," Dunbar said. "Spence [Kendrick] said, 'My radio people say that's crazy.' I told him, 'Well, your radio people don't know their ass from first base.' I put the shows out on the road, which served us well because people came out to be a part of it. We got big ad dollars and a lot of exposure we couldn't have gotten unless we spent a lot on media. It was a way to make the on-air staff very personable to our listeners, and we saved a lot of money.

"We had no numbers, no ratings, no nothing," he said. "But we had people who would show up at events. We were able to bring people to advertisers. We never went on any sales calls where we didn't come out with an order. We knew what product we had, and we knew how to please advertisers and listeners.

"All you're doing selling radio is selling fluff and air," Dunbar said. "It's BS. Look at big ad agencies with big advertisers like Kroger or something like that. They'll buy ads on fifteen stations in a market without having a clue. They're just buying numbers and thinking people will listen. We had to actually prove to [each] advertiser that people would listen to us, and they'd come into your store. Using that old thought process is what made The Ticket very, very successful. It entertained the people who listened to it and it was worth the money advertisers spent on it."

So The Ticket was almost all grown up. It had its own facility, its hosts were becoming local celebrities, and the money was starting to flow.

But things weren't all rosy, as a subtle battle was taking place behind the scenes between two distinct sports-radio philosophies.

4

WHY CONSULTANTS ARE LIKE PIGEONS

MIKE RHYNER never envisioned The Ticket as a hard-core sports station, where conversation about the Cowboys' prevent defense ruled the day. He knew that if the station had tried that approach, it would have lasted about three months—if that long.

"We knew we couldn't just be straight-up sports from the beginning," Rhyner said. "For some reason, the idea that we [wanted to] is out there, and I'm not sure why. It's probably because when we did try to wander off track in the early days we encountered some resistance from within—the guys running the station—for about the first year and a half.

"There was already a lot of that in this market when we started up this thing," he said. "Go back and take a snapshot of what was going on in sports radio around here at that time. Even though there was no full-time sports station, the 6 P.M. time slot was designated by anyone who did any talk at all for sports. You had *Sports at Six* on WBAP, *Sports Central Dallas* on KRLD and *The Sports Brothers* on KLIF.

"We had to set ourselves apart in some way. I didn't know exactly how to do that, but my instinct told me there would have to be some sort of window—however sizable that may or may not have been—to get off into other stuff when we wanted to. We did that quite a bit. We encountered resistance when we did, but we kept on doing it."

This just wasn't the way sports radio was supposed to be done. Powerhouse all-sports stations like WFAN in New York were all Xs and Os, all the time. Talking about your kid's first successful solo performance on the toilet? Talking about how bad the new Eagles album sucks? Blasphemy. Pure blasphemy.

"Certain precepts seemed to be held throughout the market, and one was you couldn't go off-track," Rhyner said. "A big assumption was that people [only] wanted to hear your opinions on the Cowboys' third-string linebacker and the salary cap. That was all they wanted. If you didn't do that, not only were you doing them a disservice, you were also not going to be successful."

Big Brother

The higher-ups at Cardinal Communications, the company Spence Kendrick had formed to run the station, weren't on board with Rhyner's habit of meandering off the aforementioned sports track. They felt someone was needed to keep the boys in line, and that someone was a consultant (who shall remain nameless) hired to critique every show on the station. His method of doing so was to fire a barrage of faxes from his home every five minutes, basically telling Rhyner, Craig Miller, George Dunham and Greg Williams that they all sucked, and then telling them why.

"I didn't know [the consultant], didn't know how this would work, and really didn't care too much," Miller said. "After a while, though, it got to where we all felt like trained monkeys trying to please him. You never saw him; he was this Big Brother, larger-than-life figure who had all these directions. He had us all thinking too much. After getting five faxes a day, a lot of which were counter-intuitive to what we were trying to do, we all realized it was a bad situation."

Rhyner said he knew Kendrick was bringing in the consultant, but he, like Miller, didn't give much thought to it. What they didn't tell him, however, was that the consultant was to be an all-pervasive and all-powerful presence, and that the management was going to believe whatever he told them.

Rhyner soon became disgusted with the constant meddling. He'd make a big production of throwing away each fax he received, stopping just short of wiping his ass with the "suggestion."

"Consultants are like pigeons," Rhyner said. "They fly in, shit all over everything and fly out.

"When he'd fax me, he'd fax the same thing to everybody else. I used to make a big public scene of going to my mailbox and getting the fax. Then I'd get to a place in the office where there were a lot of people around and everybody could see me. Then I'd wad it up and throw it over my shoulder without reading it."

Specifically, the consultant constantly complained that both *Dunham & Miller* and *The Hardline* didn't immediately go to the phones. They were supposed to introduce themselves, say hi and get to callers within the first three minutes. No playing grab-ass—just get straight to it.

Rhyner was having none of it. He wanted to use the first segment to set the stage for the day's presentation, to summarize what he and Williams were going to talk about for the next three hours, to "dip his toes in the water," if you will.

Miller felt the same way, and he was just as disgusted with the faceless entity that was making his work life miserable. "He didn't even want anybody to go by a nickname," Miller said. "There was no 'Georgio,' 'Jub-Jub,' 'The Hammer' or 'Junior.' We couldn't get off the sports path. He wanted us to do everything that would have led to our ultimate failure.

"We wanted to be funny and get off on tangents," he said. "He probably stunted our show's growth for a while."

Not that Dunham and Miller couldn't have used a little guidance in the early days. Some of the first shows—and both of them have said this—were horrific. Much of what they did at first wouldn't come close to seeing the light of day today.

Case in point was a bit they called "Stupid Trivia"—at least that's the name Miller remembers it by. Somebody would call in and give Dunham and Miller the answer to a fake trivia question; the answer was supposed to contain a funny sports name. If the answer made George and Craig laugh, they'd give the caller a fake gift.

Yeah, it's safe to say that was a pretty lame idea.

But that was a small symptom of a bigger problem that was plaguing the show, Miller said.

"That bit may have been good for a five-minute quick hit at most, but we used to do our entire three-hour show as nothing but that," Miller said. "We'd take call after call after call with funny sports names. We'd beat stuff into the ground. We had no idea how to hit and run things, no idea how to do one segment on sports, make the next one funny, and then go back to sports. We had no idea how to strike a balance—we were rudderless."

On thin ice

So the consultant sometimes had a point, when criticizing Dunham and Miller at least, but overall he was way off base. However, the hosts knew the management was listening to the recommendations. Rhyner thought he was going to be canned for sure.

"There was very lax security back in those days, with offices left open at night and confidential faxes left lying around," Rhyner said. "I saw several that alluded to when they were going to fire us. They were going to wait for our first ratings report, because they knew it would be bad, and then they could say, 'It's not working. See ya.'

"The consultant was an irritant more than anything else, but he was a big irritant," he added. "I told myself when I started this thing that I was going to do it my way. If I couldn't, I wasn't going to do it."

Right. But after all the time, work and worry Rhyner had invested, helping build the station from scratch, there was no way he was going to let an invisible consultant force him out.

"I don't know, I might have left," he said. "The thing about it, though, is they feared if I left, the other guys would be right behind me. I don't know if that would have happened, but the fact is, by then it was apparent to everybody in the business that we had a good product. It probably would have taken about a nanteenth of a second for any of us to get snapped up by somebody."

Then the first ratings came out. And they didn't look exactly like the management thought they would.

The Ticket had proven immensely, shockingly popular in a very short time.

Thoughts of firing anybody dissolved faster than a sugar cube in a cup of hot tea. And even better, Rhyner's battle with the consultant would soon end when Cardinal sold the station to SFX Broadcasting.

"The new guys came in and got rid of him," Rhyner said. "I don't remember any kind of specific celebration on my part, but I remember saying to myself, 'Now *that* was sweet.' I don't remember what I did, really, or if I did anything at all. But that was done, and the next thing was for me to impress the new ownership. It was really just a matter of clearing one hurdle and having to focus on the other."

Enter "The Laddy"

Kendrick sold Cardinal in 1995 after getting a "Godfather deal"—one he simply couldn't refuse—from SFX. This was after a period of time when industry heavyweights Infinity Broadcasting and Susquehanna Broadcasting, as well as SFX, were hovering around Kendrick, just itching for the chance to entice him into selling the station.

"By late December they were all calling, checking in," Kendrick said. "They said, 'Hey, congratulations on your latest ratings. You've done a great job building the station, blah, blah, blah.'"

Late in 1994, the FCC had started relaxing its consolidation rules. Before, a single company could only own one AM and one FM station per market. But after the relaxation, an entity could own up to 40 percent of all the stations in a given market. So the big boys were rubbing their hands together, foaming at the mouth to buy one of the fastest growing stations in America.

"We were just getting to break even on an operating basis—we didn't make money the first year," Kendrick said. "It was just getting to where it was self-sustaining. When they came in and made us a really good offer—way above what anybody thought you could get for a standalone AM station—I asked myself whether it was a good deal for my investors. After all, that's ultimately who I was responsible to. Those investors did very well."

New ownership obviously means new personnel calling the shots; that's the way it is in every business. For The Ticket, the biggest changes were a new general manager, Bob Huntley, and the man who many credit for taking the station from the crawling to the walking stage: program director Mike Thompson, a.k.a., "The Wild Irish Laddy," or just "The Laddy."

Thompson was actually given the option of keeping the consultant around, but he declined. "I met with the guy and talked to him," The Laddy said, "but I just felt like if this was going to be my show, it wasn't going to work out if he was still there. I didn't think it would have been beneficial for either of us to keep that arrangement.

"But I don't blame Spence for hiring him. That consultant had been successful in many areas of radio, and he did come up with some clever things," he said. "He served a purpose; his time was just up. As we said at The Ticket, 'Ahhh, buddy, it was time.'"

Listeners couldn't have cared less when The Laddy was brought in. He was just another suit to them. But to Rhyner and Miller, it was a huge boost for the station. The Laddy was on their side. He didn't try to muzzle *Dunham & Miller* or *The Hardline*; he gave them the freedom to take their shows in whatever direction they saw fit.

"The greatness of The Laddy was that he was our first real advocate," Rhyner said. "He was the first guy who came in and said, 'Hey, what you guys are doing is good.' He was also the first guy to ever really embrace, and shield us from, whatever static we got for doing 'guy talk.' It was on his watch that we really began to take off.

"The Laddy is one of the smartest radio guys I've ever known," Rhyner added. "He understands just about every facet of the business; he understands sales, ratings, how Arbitron works and what you can do to make it work for you. And he understands talent and coaching that talent to get the best out of it. It never hurts to be told when you do something that works, or when you do something that's good. And he would tell us that often."

"When The Laddy came in, he pointed everyone in the right direction," Miller said. "He was like, 'The show's about you guys: *your* opinions, *your* stories.' He said if you talk nothing but sports, you're going to appeal to this small audience. If you talk sports *and* about your family life, music, women, etc., you're going to appeal to everybody. That means more listeners and bigger ratings."

The Laddy's biggest moves—and examples of how his influence can still be felt more than ten years after he left the station—were firing Skip Bayless and Chuck Cooperstein, and moving Dunham and Miller to their morning shift and teaming them with Gordon Keith. He also stressed to everybody that they needed to achieve the aforementioned goal of learning to "hit and run," so to speak. Talk Cowboys for a little while, then do a funny bit, then talk Mavericks, then do guy talk about stupid billboards or whatever, then get back on the sports page. This "checkerboarding," or going back and forth between segments, is a Ticket staple to this day.

The Laddy also encouraged the hosts to get out of their comfort zone, like sending Gordo out to do bits—political polling sites, bus stations, wherever—to make *Dunham & Miller* more of a local show.

"I was blessed to have the opportunity to work with those guys," said The Laddy, who, after leaving The Ticket, worked for stations in Philadelphia, Atlanta and Los Angeles before ultimately becoming the general manager of Pittsburgh's ESPN Radio affiliate. "[Program director successor] Bruce Gilbert and I talked about that often, how we caught lightning in a bottle.

"There's a unique thing about Dallas that people don't really get," he said. "There's an industriousness, a hard-work ethic you don't find in a lot of places. The guys at the station work their asses off. And back then they weren't doing it for a lot of money. To me, in order to build that radio station, it had to be about *Dunham & Miller* and *The Hardline.*

"Did I get resistance from that? Yeah, I got it," The Laddy added. "As a matter of fact, Spence was petitioning the SFX people to fire me. I'm an average sports fan, but I'm a radio guy. Spence—with all due respect, since he's a huge reason there even is a Ticket—was a huge sports fan who didn't know a lot about radio. The best analogy I can come up with regarding him is it's like having a grandmother who's a great cook [who] then tries to open a restaurant. There's a big difference between preparing the family meal and running a restaurant."

The Laddy said Kendrick was upset because The Laddy eliminated the *In the Crease* hockey show hosted by E.J. Hradek (who now writes for ESPN.com), as well as Hank Haney's golf show. "I focused the station on Cowboys, Cowboys, Cowboys," The Laddy said. "I took off the hockey show because it was airing certain weeknights during football season. In my judgment, even though there were some good Stars stories, the way to go was to give 'em Cowboys until it hurt. I think that pissed off Spence. And he was a good buddy of Hank's, so he was really pissed when I eliminated that show.

"Anyway, he was a real sports nut, and he thought I was taking The Ticket away from being a sports station. The problem in talk radio, whether it's political or sports talk, is that when it's too focused on topic, when nothing happens, you're screwed. The way you build a successful station is through your guys, your personalities.

"I knew the station had to be great 365 days a year. And I also knew the devotion we were lucky enough to get from the P1s, the Day One guys who supported the station," The Laddy added. "We had to make sure that when there wasn't really anything going on in the sports world, we could still make those guys laugh."

It was that approach that poised The Ticket for take-off. The Laddy had lit the fuse; ignition would occur thanks to the great Bruce Gilbert.

5

THE NEXT LEVEL

THE TICKET has evolved from a bunch of guys flailing about and playing radio to a streamlined entity whose hosts deliver a well-developed balance of sports and shtick with succinct timing. It's a balance that isn't forced

or formulaic, but rather "organically grown," in a sense. Each host has refined his own craft to the point that it's almost effortless. Of course, it helps that most of them have performed their shows three or four thousand times—maybe triple that number in the case of Norm Hitzges.

"We're all better talk-show hosts," said George Dunham. "There's a certain art to presenting a talk show—it's not rocket science, but you need to be concise, make a point and have a purpose for what you're saying. Some of the time in the early days, we didn't know what we were going to talk about. We may not be any better to-day—that's up to the listener to decide."

On the rise

The station first started really growing its "sea legs," so to speak, barely a year into its existence. The guys knew they had started finding their way, and ratings were increasing dramatically. One host, Craig Miller, said he knew The Ticket was on its way to suc-cess a mere seven months after it first took to the air.

"A lot of guys point to our first Guys' Night Out in July of '94," Miller said. "We were all expecting about fifty people to show up, but hundreds showed up. And they were all very passionate about the station. I think that's when a lot of us [realized] the station was going to be really big."

And when it became apparent that the station was going to be a hit, it would have been understandable for the on-air talent to pick up the phone and flaunt their success to some of the people who had told them it would never work. The same people who, as Mike Rhyner said, had patted them on the heads and told them they'd still have their old jobs after they saw the folly of this thing.

"It wasn't so much picking up the phone to anyone in particular, but we've said that kind of thing in so many words about, oh, a billion times on the air, figuring they'd either be listening or word would get back to them," Miller said. "I made sure that on the air I told them how I felt."

The paychecks started getting better as ratings improved. Although of course nobody wanted to get into specifics as to how much they make, suffice it to say nobody on the air is going to have to sweat the price of gas anytime soon.

"I think in the first two years, if I remember correctly, Greggo and I were the lowest-paid hosts," Miller said. "They made some really weird hires; they brought in Kate Delany, 'The Sports Princess,' to work nights, and she was making more than anybody.

"But after five or six years, we started making a fair wage," he said. "In the early days we were making a lesser wage just because it was a startup and we didn't really care what we were making. We were just glad to be in Dallas working at an all-sports station."

With success, of course, comes recognition, and all The Ticket hosts are fairly large Dallas-area celebrities today. The seemingly endless stream of local appearances played a huge role in that, of course, plus the fact that the station became so incredibly popular.

"It was pretty cool," Miller said. "I started getting [recognition] in the first year or two, which shows how much the listeners were into it from the early days. When somebody says, 'I hate to bother you, but I just wanted to say I enjoy your show,' I tell them—and it's the honest truth—that I never care if somebody comes up to me, unless they're an ass.

"When they tell me they enjoy the show, I'm always really appreciative of that, because it means we still have a job," he said. "When the day comes when nobody comes up and says that, then I know we're in trouble."

A lot of the credit for the rise of The Ticket goes to two men: Mike Thompson, "The Laddy," and his successor as program director, Bruce Gilbert. The Laddy, as discussed in the previous chapter, was the one who, in large part, freed the hosts from the shackles of constant talk of Xs and Os, and moved them to the realm of "guy talk."

"About six months into my time at The Ticket, I started noticing the trend of how long the listeners were staying with us," said The

Laddy, who took over as Ticket program director in 1995 after the station was sold to SFX. "I also noticed that people in the media were listening to our station—guys like Kidd Kraddick and Randy Galloway. When [then-Cowboys head coach] Barry Switzer referred to us in a press conference"—The Musers had a bit where they'd set an over/under on the number of times Switzer would curse—"it was apparent that we had become 'The Little Engine that Could.' We had become viral, and that term hadn't even been invented yet.

"But I also knew in my gut rather than just my ear," The Laddy continued. "When I chuckled, or I laughed, I was having a great time listening to my radio station. I wasn't bored."

Ultimately, The Laddy said, he told the hosts their efforts would finally start paying off in the form of bonuses and incentives for reaching certain ratings benchmarks. "I still do this today," he said. "When contract time was up I kept little Post-It notes. In the middle of a show, as the hosts were talking, I'd come in the studio and put a note in front of them. On it I had written '7K,' or '8K,' whatever it was. Those were the days they started realizing they had a hand in their income through their hard work.

"Now they're all making big money and they deserve it," said The Laddy, who left The Ticket for a station in Philadelphia, then worked at stations in Los Angeles and Atlanta before becoming the general manager of Pittsburgh's ESPN Radio affiliate. "Those guys are still very special to me. I like to think I laid some of the foundation, but Bruce built the house. He really took the station to the next level."

The Great "Zhil-Behr"

The Laddy isn't the only one who credits Bruce Gilbert with finding that "next level" for the station (whatever that really means), but Gilbert doesn't want any part of those kudos.

"You're talking about a radio station that's had an incredible following and amazing success," Gilbert said. "It's ridiculous to think any one person makes that much of a difference. While I appreciate what everybody says about me 'taking it to the next level,' I'm not sure what that means, either.

"I was extremely fortunate in my timing in that it was the perfect storm," he said. "The company that owned [The Ticket] had had it a couple of years; the guys who were making it happen on the air were sort of struggling along through several owners. I was just fortunate enough to get in there when it was starting to solidify. Everybody was sort of clamoring for direction, if you will. My job was to chart a course, to figure out where we wanted to be and how we were going to get there.

"The reality is they figured that out on their own, and they made it happen on their own because they were the talent," Gilbert continued. "The 'next level' happened because we all challenged each other; not because of what I did or any other one person did. It was a group of incredibly creative people who weren't afraid to try or do anything.

"That, to me, was the secret."

"Trepidation" is too strong a word to describe what Gilbert was feeling upon his arrival to The Ticket in 1997, but "apprehension" isn't strong enough. He said he didn't know what the hell he was getting into. Nobody knew the future of sports radio, which was still basically in its infancy as a radio format. There was a big question mark across the industry as to whether or not it could really work.

"It's much like the doubts surrounding ESPN when it first came on in 1979," Gilbert said. "I remember review after review saying, 'Sports twenty-four hours a day? Seriously? How are they going to do that?'

"Radio was kind of in that place in 1997," he said. "People were doing sports radio, but no one really knew for sure if it was going to work. The apprehension on my part was whether I was getting into a format that wouldn't have any legs.

"To be honest, the first month I was there I didn't get it," Gilbert said. "I was a damn Yankee coming down from up north. I remember listening and saying to myself, 'Who are these guys and what are they talking about?' It was a very different-sounding radio station.

"But then I realized how lucky I was to have that," Gilbert added. "That was absolutely what set it apart: I realized how unique it was. I can't say I realized at the time that I was a part of something special. You don't know that in the moment—you're just doing your job."

When Gilbert first arrived, the success of The Ticket was primarily centered on *The Hardline* and football season. Gilbert's main challenge was to make The Ticket more than a one-show, seasonal radio station. The entire station did well during the fall, and *The Hardline* did well whenever it was on the air, but the goal was to make the numbers work across all seasons and all shows.

The first thing Gilbert had to do was answer that "clamoring for direction" that everyone in the station was feeling.

"They had had a lot of different owners, and a lot of different bosses under those different owners," Gilbert said. "After a while, if you're an on-air talent, there comes a point where you've been told so much, you don't know whether to scratch your armpit, wind your watch or pick your nose. There was no clarity.

"I'm not saying anyone expressed that verbatim; that's just a feeling I had," he said. "In order to be a good leader, you have to have people who want to be led. That was my perception of them. They were like, 'Show us what you've got. What's your vision?' Fortunately, much of what I thought we should do with the station was already in their minds. I didn't think of anything unique; they knew where they wanted to take it, how they wanted to grow. They knew they wanted to be more of a lifestyle and relatable radio station, and we were able to paint the picture together."

Gilbert said all he wanted to do was get higher ratings for the station. But he had no idea how to do so. "I was sitting there listening to these really unique shows and thinking about the principles I had learned in other formats in other markets. I asked myself, 'Do any of them apply? Do none of them apply?'

"I tried to methodically apply all the things I thought would benefit our ratings," he said. "Instead of me telling the talent what to do and what not to do, we implemented some basic radio principles that these guys lacked simply because they had never been taught any of them. It wasn't rocket science. It was just a matter of everybody understanding how to generate ratings."

One method was building "cume," or cumulative audience. Cume is similar to a newspaper's circulation. It's defined as "the different or unduplicated persons or households listening during a specified period." And one of the ways to drive cume was to saturate the streets like no other station in Dallas-Fort Worth.

"We're fortunate that we had the kind of staff that loved being out and meeting people," Gilbert said. "Every time we did that, it was advertising for our radio station. Maybe they had heard a little bit about the station while they were at a roadshow or some other Ticket event, and maybe they'd start listening a little more.

"You've got to get them in the door," he said. "Cume is the same as if you had a retail store when somebody comes in. Time spent listening is the same as time spent in your store. Once we got them to listen, the key was to get them to listen longer. We identified many different ways we felt we could do that, either through really great teasing for what we were going to talk about after commercial, or great storytelling.

"More importantly, it was just having great content all the time, talking about stuff people cared about," Gilbert added. "Everybody embraced that, and we started seeing results."

Multiple personalities

Just about every time The Ticket did something that required some sort of listener participation, from roadshows to events like Charity Challenge on Ice or Ticketstock, or even selling "Best of" CDs, the reaction was astounding. One of the reasons, Gilbert believes, is that the station had become ingrained in its audience's psyche.

"I've been in radio about thirty years. I know it works; it's a great, emotional medium that touches people," Gilbert said. "But The Ticket was something completely different in the sense that its listeners didn't just like the station, they were ambassadors for—and fanatics of—the station. More particularly, of the talent. The Ticket as a business was a combination of the DNA of all the hosts.

"It worked because everybody on that station was relatable to somebody," he said. "You either identified yourself with the curmudgeonly Mike Rhyner, or you were the redneck Texan like Greg Williams, or you were the clean-cut college guy like Dunham and Miller, or you were the frat guy Gordon Keith who always peed in the punch bowl. And if you weren't one of those people, you had a brother, father, uncle, cousin or friend who was.

"The Ticket was all of those personalities combined," Gilbert added. "It was a phenomenon; it was one of those special moments that can't be duplicated, could never be replicated and no one could ever design it if they tried."

Gilbert said he knew The Ticket had not only become a huge success locally, but had also influenced sports radio as a whole, when he would go to national radio conventions or trade shows. Time after time after time, radio station executives would ask him what the hell he was doing and how the hell he was doing it.

"Everybody wants that magic bullet, that secret potion," Gilbert said. "They wanted to know how we designed our format clocks or what content we were talking about. But it was [always] the people.

"The station had an irreverence about it," he said. "We worked hard but didn't take ourselves seriously. And that's the answer I would give all these people at the trade shows. But people would roll their eyes and say, 'Oh, you don't want to give out any secrets.' No—there were no secrets. I told them to come to Dallas and listen for a week. Chances are they wouldn't get it.

"But it works in Dallas-Fort Worth because they relate to the people who live there. They're relevant, and they're irreverent in the way they present."

The bunker mentality

The kudos and ratings wins were great, but they also scared the hell out of everybody at The Ticket. The on-air talent particularly tried to maintain a "bunker mentality," to keep their heads down and keep doing their jobs without becoming conceited and lazy. They kept telling themselves they weren't really that great; even though people loved them today, they could just as easily hate them tomorrow.

That approach was severely tested when they officially hit The Big Time—when they became No. 1 in the most coveted demographic in radio: men aged 25–54.

"It was fun ascending, but it scared us to death when we achieved that ranking," Gilbert said. "We were looking at each other saying, 'Holy shit. How do we keep this?'

"What we realized was we needed to stop putting pressure on ourselves and just do what we do, keep looking for unique twists and continue to be relevant and smart," he said. "To use a football analogy, one of the things we never stopped doing was blocking and tackling. We didn't get so caught up in the razzle-dazzle of the gadget plays that we stopped doing the basics.

"And I give the guys a lot of credit for that, because that's the hard part; the grinding, day-in and day-out Xs and Os of a three- or four-hour show," Gilbert added. "People don't realize the work and discipline involved in that. I give all the on-air guys and producers behind the scenes the credit for making sure everybody understood the importance of the Xs and Os."

Of course, not every single thing The Ticket touched turned to gold during that time. There were some duds along the way, such as certain roadshows where nobody showed up. And on-air, there were always some failed bits scattered around; that just goes with the territory.

"There were certainly several things that we tried that didn't work, but those are the things you forget," Gilbert said. "We always knew the only way to succeed was to sometimes fail."

"All of those things were part of the process," he added. "What would have led us to fail would have been to sit still. That started at the top with [Ticket general manager] Dan Bennett, who's one of the greatest people I've ever worked for. He gave us the freedom to just keep trying.

"We challenged each other to keep trying stuff, throw it against the wall, because that's what helped make the station a success. Some stuff sticks and some doesn't."

Three big moves

During his time at The Ticket, Gilbert made three huge moves that still reverberate at the station. He fired the incendiary Rocco Pendola, replaced him with the venerable Norm Hitzges, and hired Bob and Dan to take the noon–3 P.M. slot.

The Pendola firing will be covered in more detail later. For now, let's just say he wasn't a good guy "in the room." He wasn't exactly one of the guys. Randy Moss wasn't very good for some of the rooms he was a part of, either, but if he scored twenty-five touchdowns, you can be damn sure nobody would be getting rid of him. Unfortunately for Pendola, he didn't cross the goal line nearly enough to offset the disruptive force he had become within the otherwise nurturing bosom of The Little Ticket.

"We gave Rocco an extremely generous period of time to prove he could be successful," Gilbert said. "The reality was he wasn't generating the same kind of ratings as the rest of the station. You couple that with the chemistry issue, and it was a very difficult decision. I thought he was a very talented guy, but it wasn't the right fit."

Gilbert's pairing of the vastly different Bob Sturm and Dan McDowell to replace Pendola was, as he puts it, a "mad chemistry project" that has lasted more than ten years and constantly generated powerful ratings during the mid-day time slot.

"There was no way anyone could predict these two guys would

do a show well together," Gilbert said. "They had no history, but their personalities offset each other well enough to create some kind of radio magic. I'm proud they're still on the station."

And as for the last of Gilbert's big moves, bringing Hitzges to The Ticket helped the station assume a level of credibility among hardcore sports talk fans that they hadn't seen since the departure of Chuck Cooperstein.

"I was a huge fan of his, and he was kind of on an island, trying to do sports on a station that wasn't all sports," Gilbert said, referring to KLIF, where Hitzges worked before coming to The Ticket. "You could say he didn't fit the mold of the rest of the guys, but what he brought was a heightened level of credibility. The timing of that was pretty much in line with ESPN Radio coming into the marketplace.

"Our market research showed we had a lot of credibility, but that was the right time to amp it up, and Norm did that in one quick move."

All grownsed up

Not only did Gilbert successfully reshape the on-air roster and oversee the station when it emerged as a ratings powerhouse, he also had a hand in The Ticket's evolution from mere fun and yuks to being a true touchstone of the Metroplex.

The bitter and confused aftermath of the terrorist attacks of September 11, 2001 inflamed passions throughout the country, and Dallas-Fort Worth was obviously no different. All The Ticket hosts, thanks to a decision made by Gilbert, had the chance to act as mature commentators, voicing the confusion and frustration of their listeners. Instead of simply throwing all Ticket programming to a news network, as was his prerogative, Gilbert stayed on the air and let his guys feel their way through an unprecedented time in American history.

Below is an excerpt from a September 27, 2001 *Dallas Observer* article by Eric Celeste.

It was at that point that the hosts on the air and the ones who followed took off their 'yuk monkey' masks and revealed themselves as deserving commentators in the subsequent search for understanding.

The Ticket would provide pitch-perfect coverage of the terrorist tragedy: heartfelt, comforting, angry, honest. Callers shared their horror; hosts expressed equal parts fury, understanding and confusion; Barry Switzer cried. It was, for the P1s, P2s and even the marginal P3s, a town hall of the airwaves where they could join the cacophony of aftermath.

It's this sense of frankness that has always run through The Ticket and made it so popular. In a word, then, they were honest in their response, in their love of fart jokes and country and everything in between. This no-bullshit edict is what makes the station successful, and it is what made its coverage unique and appropriate.

In a time when America had no idea when it would be OK to laugh again, The Ticket helped its listeners feel their way through an incredibly difficult period, and in the process they formed an exponentially stronger bond with that audience than they had ever enjoyed.

The tree house

The guys had grown up, but not grown out of their propensity for bathroom humor. Soon they would be the same irreverent group they had always been, and at times they caused a lot of headaches for Gilbert.

Dan McGraw, of the *Fort Worth Weekly*, wrote in the July 25, 2002 edition of the magazine that Gilbert was "the parent who must occasionally go into the tree house and create some order out of the chaos." Many times Gilbert had to bring one of the hosts to the principal's office for crossing the line.

"I had to do that with virtually everybody on the staff at one time," Gilbert said. "There were probably a few more of those conversations with Gordon than anybody else. I don't think that surprises anybody; Gordo is really free-spirited and incredibly creative. He was really good at staying right along that line, but occasionally he jumped over it.

"The problem is, that line moves all the time," Gilbert continued. "It's subjective to some extent. The only time I would sit anyone down is when it became more objective, it became blatant. We tried to define it as best we could without confining the guys, but when something couldn't be interpreted any other way than in the hard-core, dirty way they said it, that didn't put me in a position where I could defend it."

Sometimes one of the hosts would make a blatantly sexual re-mark, other times he'd say something that could be construed as being racially insensitive. But more often than not, problems stemmed from the redundancy of a comment, such as when it was made into a drop and played over and over again. Other times the hosts would simply stay on a subject too long. Although Gilbert said he had to confront just about every host at one time or another, it didn't happen too often because they were good at walking up to the line, sticking their toe just on the other side of it, then quickly bringing it back. They knew how to hit it and quit it, so to speak.

"When you have that kind of creative group of people who are very open, honest and raw, they're going to say some things that offend people—even offend me," Gilbert said. "We had to try and balance that, because we didn't want to stop pushing it. Every day we offended people; that's part of what made it successful. But we had to manage the level with which we were comfortable doing that. Were we being real or just blatantly outrageous?

"For me the measuring stick was the gratuitous nature of it," he said. "When I felt guys were doing something just because they felt they could—saying, 'I'm on The Ticket so I can say this'—that's when I got particularly irked. I wanted it to be natural and in con-text. If there was a story that called for a little more colorful com-mentary, I was OK with it in the proper context. But when guys started doing stuff just because they thought they could, that's when they paid a visit to my office. I didn't tolerate that stuff."

Gilbert couldn't come up with a specific incident where a host did something so egregious that he had to sit him down, but he did recall an instance where he had to bring someone into his office for a completely different reason. There was an unnamed board operator whose funk permeated the studio—a BO with BO, if you will. Nobody wanted to confront the guy, so that pleasant task fell to Gilbert.

"He just plain stank," Gilbert said. "It kept escalating to the point where I had to call him in. I said to him, 'I don't know how to tell you this, but you stink. Everybody's noticed it. When you leave a room, the rest of you doesn't leave for another three minutes.'

"It was obvious he was a clean guy; I mean, his hair always looked clean so he apparently showered," he said. "He came back to me two days later and said, 'Yeah, I kind of have a problem doing my laundry. I put all my clothes in a pile and grab something on the way out the door.' That fixed the problem."

Time to go

Gilbert's tenure at The Ticket ended in 2003 when he left to oversee the ESPN Radio network. He has since taken the CEO position at Red Zebra Broadcasting, a nascent, Virginia-based network owned by Daniel Snyder that has broadcasts of Snyder's Washington Redskins as its centerpiece.

Gilbert said the most important thing he learned in Dallas was that if you hire smart, talented, good people and let them do their jobs, the results can be amazing. The accolades you receive as a result can be even more amazing.

"I really get embarrassed when people say I had this or that to do with The Ticket," Gilbert said. "I just don't believe that. It was the most impressive display of guys working together that I've ever been a part of. I don't deserve the credit for that. Dan Bennett deserves it. He was the type of leader who said to me, 'It's your station. Just keep me informed. Find a way to harness their creativity and keep it in check, but let them be who they are.'

"Dan said, 'We don't ever want anybody at The Ticket we have to kick in the ass. We only want guys who we have to pull back,'" Gilbert said. "That's a great position to be in.

"It was really hard—day in and day out, month in and month out—to continue to reinvent The Ticket," he said. "I'm not saying I did that; I mean for all of us. I don't know how much longer I could have motivated the guys, because they were so damn good. I knew they were in good hands with [my successor] Jeff Catlin.

"But it was extremely hard to leave that station. I loved all those guys, and I still do. I have an incredible amount of respect for what they've done," Gilbert said. "I had an offer that was too good to pass up from ESPN, but I had Ticket withdrawals for a year. That was a time in my life that no longer exists, and I'm not going to get bogged down in it. But inevitably I talk to all the guys at least once a year at the Super Bowl, and immediately there's that connection and respect and appreciation for each other.

"Not to get too overly corny and sentimental, but there's a fondness there that will never leave my heart. It wasn't all strawberries, roses and wine; we had our share of difficulties. But it was an incredibly special ride."

6

BEHIND THE SCENES

I N THE NEXT SECTION you'll get to know the stars of the show: the hosts. This chapter, though, is devoted to the guys who aren't in the spotlight five days a week, but who, in their own way, are still vital to the smooth operation of the presentation.

The Big Guy

Dan Bennett is at the top of The Ticket food chain. As general manager, he's the one who's ultimately accountable for the success or failure of the station on his watch.

He inspects everything, from expenses, promotions and media to branding and sales. He doesn't involve himself in the day-to-day aspect of programming, however, as those responsibilities go to program director Jeff Catlin.

Bennett started his career in radio as a sixteen-year-old DJ at WREN-AM in his hometown of Topeka, Kansas. By the time he was twenty-two he was the station's program director, and by twenty-seven he was its general manager.

In 1983, when Bennett's wife received a job offer in Dallas, the couple moved to the Metroplex. Bennett worked as a DJ at KPLX-FM for six months and was hired as the program director at KLIF in May of 1984. It was at that time that Bennett and other KLIF management began to look at programming options for the struggling station, and by 1986 the format changed to talk radio. Bennett was promoted to station manager at KLIF in 1993, then became the general manager of both KLIF and The Ticket when Susquehanna bought The Ticket in 1996. He still maintains his KLIF/Ticket duties today, and he also runs two Cumulus-owned stations in Greenville, Texas.

When he got to The Ticket, he saw a station that was flying high on one side and being run into the ground on the other.

"I had a lot of respect for what The Ticket had done. I really felt the on-air side was impressive," Bennett said. "But the business and sales sides weren't. The Ticket was losing a lot of money.

"We saw The Ticket as a very viable product that just wasn't sold or run well as a business," he said. "We were able to quickly turn it from a big money loser to a money maker—literally in the first month. We addressed expenses that were out of control and started charging for ads what the station was worth. It had been way undervalued."

Bennett cleaned house in the sales department from top to bottom, helping to take a station that had lost $100,000 the month before Susquehanna bought it and turning it into a cash flow–positive business. Bennett, sales manager Jim Quirk and business controller Joan Leonard comprised the team that turned it around for The Ticket.

"We had to eliminate some positions—which we did—and had to explain to the staff that we were losing money and why we were about to do what we were about to do," Bennett said. "You had to get people who understood that The Ticket was a lot more valuable to advertisers than what they were selling it for. Once we accomplished that, the station went on an almost meteoric rise in advertising income every year."

It's a rise that culminated in The Ticket being the No. 1 billing radio station in Dallas-Fort Worth in 2007. Now *that's* turning the thing around.

But even though Bennett has overseen The Ticket's transition from bleeding money to raking it in, that doesn't mean the station's content doesn't still make him cringe at times. Thanks to an elaborate delay system, though, Bennett doesn't have to

The Real Dan Bennett.

stress over the hosts nearly as much as he used to. The system lets producers dump content up to six times in a row, a quantum leap from the single seven-second delay the station formerly used. That ability to eliminate up to thirty-six seconds of content is bigger than it sounds—huge, actually. And there's even another failsafe, a red button in Catlin's office that serves as "the dump of last resort." It's safe to say the station goes to the extreme to protect its license.

"First of all, creative, brilliant people will always test the limits; push it right up to the line," Bennett said. "I don't wince as much as I used to, because we now have a system that catches things that shouldn't get on the air. Plus, I think the guys have really improved their judgment, especially in the last few years, regarding what's acceptable and what's not."

But he doesn't have to deal with the inmates of The Ticket asylum on a daily basis. That honor/beatdown goes to program director Jeff Catlin.

The Catman of the Americas

Catlin is the one charged with overseeing the content of the station, from soup to nuts, beginning to end, A to Z. He doesn't tell the guys what to talk about, but he definitely has to ride herd over everything that happens.

"My job is to be the guy at the back of the boat keeping my hand on the rudder," Catlin said. "If I need to I'll make a little course correction. But I trust the guys to do the right thing, and they know that."

Catlin grew up in Arlington never thinking about making a career in radio. He was going to be a musician in a metal band, but something happened to derail those plans. He was working part-time at Fatso's Burgers and Blues, where one of his musician friends ran the soundboard and Catlin was the backup. One night his friend didn't want to work because he thought the gig was lame; it was Emmitt Smith's radio show on 1190 AM, which was broadcasting from Fatso's that night.

"I met the guys from 1190 and I don't even know how it came up, but I asked them about an internship," Catlin said. "I knew how to run a mixing board, so it would be a natural. I was just throwing it out there, and they said, 'Come on out to the studio.'"

Catlin was given an internship at the station, working the morning show. Every weekday he arrived at 5:30 A.M. and starting pulling sports reports, business news and other information from the news wire to give to the hosts. He'd leave at nine, then drive to Fort Worth for his "real" job, editing copy for a company that produced TV guides for newspapers. Then he'd go back home, get up and do the whole thing over again. This went on for about six months until 1190 offered him the 11 A.M.–4 P.M. board shift: twenty-five hours a week, five bucks an hour.

"I was married at the time and told my wife that I needed to figure out whether I wanted to do this or not," Catlin said. "So I quit the other job. One thing led to another and I started working forty hours a week and making three more bucks an hour. I worked weekends as well."

Pretty soon he knew he wanted to make a career out of radio. Working on a show with one of his favorite Dallas Cowboys from childhood, wide receiver Tony Hill, helped him realize it. He would soon hear of a new sports station starting up called The Ticket.

"I didn't know anything else about the station and I didn't care," Catlin said. "But I loved sports and I knew I wanted to be a part of it. I sent my resume in, and when I didn't hear anything for a while I started to get kind of pissed.

"I finally got a call to interview to be Coop's [Chuck Cooperstein's] producer," he said. "I did a phone interview with Chuck, then I heard it was between me and somebody else. The other guy got it and I thought it was bullshit; I knew I could do it."

The station had only been on-air for a month, and already *The Hardline* had gone through two producers. Mike Rhyner knew Catlin, so he asked Catlin if he'd do it.

"Mike asked me if I would be interested in being a board operator for their show just in case the producer position became filled," Catlin said. "But I wasn't interested in that.

"A few more weeks went by and I didn't hear anything, but I finally ended up getting an interview with a long-lost Ticket exec at The Men's Club," he said. "Here I am interviewing for a professional job at a gentlemen's club! I don't even remember what we talked about—*The Three Stooges* and whatever else. There were girls dancing, we were having a beer, and here I am trying to explain to him what I've done and why I want the job. And that still wasn't enough.

"I had to go back a couple of weeks later to talk to Rhyner and Greg," Catlin said. "Greg goes, 'Yeah, I remember you. I don't think I like you.' And I go, 'Yeah, I know you, and I don't think I like you either.'

"Mike was OK; he just felt he was at a different station in life than me, and he was," Catlin continued. "I just remember wondering if I could work with Greg because he was such a dick."

But Catlin got the job and soon started working as producer for

The Hardline. He was only making about $20,000, but it was decent enough money.

"The internship showed me that I loved radio, and that led me to The Ticket," Catlin said. "At that point, in both places I got an opportunity I wouldn't have had otherwise to show what I could do. I got the chance to bust my ass and create value by developing my natural talents."

Catlin would eventually leave to be program director of a station in Kansas City for two and a half years before returning to The Ticket as program director in 2003.

He's got stroke

Yes, Catlin has the power to fire any of the hosts or other on-air staff members, just in case you were wondering. But a decision like that, he said, is never made independently. He'll always have input from Dan Bennett and other members of management.

"By the time you get to a situation like that, it's a far-gone situation," Catlin said. "It's not like you walk into a room one day and tell somebody they're gone.

"If I have to sit across from somebody and fire them, and I can't look them in the eye and do it in good conscience and not feel bad about it, then I haven't done my job as a manager," he said. "What I mean by that is, if I haven't taken the time to sit with them one, two or three times to try and point out where I think they're falling short, and give them the tools and coaching they need to get back up to snuff in a reasonable amount of time, then I don't feel I've done my job correctly. But if I have done that, then I have no problem and it should be no surprise.

"But when it comes to the show hosts, I don't have to worry about them," Catlin said. "Our jobs are the same: to generate ratings for the radio station. Those guys, whether they're a host, yuk monkey, board op or producer, their job is the same. If they don't do their jobs, I haven't done mine.

"I don't come in here every morning thinking if something goes wrong I have to fire somebody. My job is to create an environment where all [the hosts] have to worry about is to come in, be entertaining and informative and do their shows."

That doesn't mean there aren't times when he has to discipline or ride the hosts. There'll be times Catlin has to bring a host in his office and get in his face. There are other times he'll pat a host on the back. After all, if a manager does nothing but yell at his employees all the time, it's only a matter of time before that approach begins to fall on deaf ears.

"I try to walk a balance between encouragement and being a dick," Catlin said. "And I will be a dick when I have to be. But I've mellowed out a lot—especially since I was producing *The Hardline*.

"When I get so upset with somebody that I feel I have to yell, it's either because they've gone totally against something I've asked them to do, or they've been extremely irresponsible on-air, and they've done it repeatedly.

"Or it's where one of the shows is getting too selfish, without looking at the big picture of the station," Catlin said. "The Ticket comes first, period. It's bigger than any one person—no matter who it is.

"When I do [yell] I think it's effective because it startles them and gets their attention. But sometimes that's needed; sometimes people need a two-by-four to the head. I'm the same way."

Keeping his ears listening

Catlin, of course, can't listen to every minute of every broadcast day. He depends on people like assistant program director Mark "Friedo" Friedman, the promotions director and others to help him keep tabs on what's happening on the station.

"I have a good handle as to what's going on," Catlin said. "If I miss something, a producer will let me know. I don't ever want my boss to come to me with something I didn't already know about. I don't ever want him to come to me and me sound like a dumbass.

"But I trust all the hosts. I've been here about fourteen years, and when I was gone for a little while I was still plugged in to the station," he said. "When you work with people this long on a day-to-day basis, you just know. My job's not to program their shows; that's theirs. Mine's to program the station. If I get caught up in every detail of what their thought process is of every single segment of every single show, I'm micro-managing. They're hugely successful, talented people. They don't need that.

Big Brother is watching

Considering how close The Ticket hosts take it to the line of what's acceptable and what's not from a "decency" standpoint, you'd think the station would be near the top of the Federal Communications Commission's speed dial list. But Catlin said that's not the case. In fact, the station has only been formally investigated twice.

In the studio hangs a list of words and terms that were deemed verboten by Ticket management. This was put up after the FCC started cracking down on TV and radio stations nationwide in light of the Janet Jackson "wardrobe malfunction" during halftime of Super Bowl XXXVIII in 2004. Although they've strayed from strict adherence over the last few years as scrutiny has somewhat abated, it's still funny to look at.

Here it is:

Words that are OUT—any words or descriptions of excretory functions or organs.

Labia, nipple, douche (douchey), I wanna bang you, bitch, jerking off, repro man, Overcusser, pissing (verb), wiener, Jesus, Jesus Christ, goddamn, she's a bitch, F off or F you, penis, vag, sister's stinky box, toss the salad, Norm's sex montage, 69, rectum, a-hole, bleeps [it got so bad that they couldn't play bleeped-out audio], ten-inch wiener, bastard bitch, jarring BMs, tea-bag.

"One time they gave us a ruling that what we did wasn't obscene—that was after one of Corby's 'Overcusser' segments in 2004," Catlin said. "The other time someone called them and said Rhyner said 'shit.' He didn't; it was stupid. He was simulating the sound of a drum and then happened to say 'it' at the end. The first one was dismissed, the second one was abandoned.

"We can't record every minute of every day," he said. "We don't keep anything unless we think we'll need it for some reason, like if someone talks about a client, says something we think will be a problem, we dump something, there's a heated exchange, or it's funny. Those are the reasons we archive stuff; not because the FCC might come back eight months later and want to hear the Overcusser."

"Do we do stuff for shock value? Do we pander? Do we pound something into the ground? Yes we do," Catlin said. "This comes under the heading of drops. They can't keep doing it over and over and over again. The one that I hate is 'I have a name for my penis.' The problem is, those are funny and can be entertaining if they're hit-and-run. When it gets played six times in a show, I have a problem with it. And that's when I'll step in."

Catlin said he tries not to call during a show to voice his concern with a bit and/or direction of conversation unless something is happening that could put the station's license in peril.

"If I call the hotline and bitch, it's because I've told them two or three times and they've either chosen not to listen to me, or they think 'This time it's OK,' or they're being egged on by somebody, or for whatever reason they're not taking what I said seriously," Catlin said. "I'll get their attention, and they'll tell everybody else around them about it. Then I've done my job."

It's a job he's done well, as The Ticket's ratings have continued to strengthen during his time at the helm. But every effective leader has someone at his side helping him. In the case of Catlin, that person is Friedo.

He always produces

Mark Friedman is best known to Ticket listeners as the producer of *The Norm Hitzges Show*. Like his producing counterparts Mike Fernandez (*Dunham & Miller*), Tom Gribble (*BaD Radio*) and Danny Balis (*The Hardline*), Friedman's main job is to keep the show on track.

Before every show, the producer and host(s) have a meeting to plan how the program will stay on the rails that particular day. Here's an example of the type of conversation Friedo and Hitzges have during theirs:

MARK: Do we have enough Cowboys today?

NORM: Yeah, way too much.

MARK: You know, the way the guests are scheduled today kind of sucks.

NORM: Yeah, it does.

MARK: Do you want to stick with the Cowboys in the first and third segments, or bump one?

NORM: I might talk about the All-Star thing and bump the Cowboys to 10:50.

MARK: What's your take on the All-Star thing? [This concerned Mark Cuban and Jerry Jones reportedly teaming up to try to bring the NBA All-Star Game to Jerry's new stadium in Arlington.]

NORM: From what I can tell, everything else would be held at American Airlines Center: the dunk contest, the three-point contest, all the pyrotechnics where people can't get out because the arena's on fire.

MARK: The city [of Dallas] didn't give Cuban an arena; they gave [Stars owner Tom] Hicks and [then-Mavericks owner Ross Jr.] Perot an arena, then he bought it. I'd be more upset if one of them wanted to take an NHL or NBA All-Star Game out of Dallas. Anyway, you have enough for Wash? [Rangers manager Ron Washington visits with Norm weekly.]

NORM: Yeah.

MARK: As a defensive guy, [Rangers pitcher Vicente] Padilla's got to fucking kill him, to watch how slow that guy works.

NORM: Yeah, but some nights he doesn't...

MARK: Norm, the other night they timed it. There was a five-minute stretch where he was facing Carlos Pena, and there had only been six pitches thrown. It's frustrating. Speaking of baseball, I'm going to pat you on the back. Do you realize how hot you are in baseball right now?

NORM: Yeah.

MARK: You leave the country [Norm had just returned from a trip to Belize], you leave me a message that you're flying blind because you don't have an Internet connection, and you go undefeated that day.

NORM: It was amazing; I got so little information. The power went out all the time. That's the thing about doing this from my house; I've got all kinds of stuff I can get a hold of. Take this, for instance, Friedo: I don't know why, but Cincinnati and Atlanta have played twenty-seven games over the last three-plus years, and they're over twenty-two of the twenty-seven games. It doesn't matter who pitches—they just get lit up. [Tom] Glavine goes against [Edinson] Volquez today; they've both been terrific this season, but I bet the final score is 9–7 or something like that. [NOTE: Not so much. The final score of that game was Cincinnati 3, Atlanta 2.]

And on it goes, an exchange of ideas that leads right up to the moment when Norm has to go into the studio to mix with The Musers.

By the time the actual show starts, most of Friedman's work has already been completed. He talks to Norm on-air some, of course, tracks breaking news and talks to callers, making sure only the good ones get on. He'll also occasionally feed Hitzges ideas for interview questions or show topics. He makes those suggestions by either talking into a microphone that goes directly into Norm's headset or sending instant messages via computer.

On this particular day he was able to take time during the show to describe to some spare writer how he got to The Ticket. And it's one of the most unlikely stories you'll find of anyone who works at the station.

Friedman grew up in Dallas and had absolutely no desire to ever get into radio. In fact, he paid his way through college by working at a restaurant and was ultimately approached by the restaurant's owner about going in as partners in a Rowlett convenience store. Friedman didn't have a lot of money, but it didn't matter. The man wanted somebody he could trust, and Friedo was it. The man offered to let him work for his equity in the store.

It was through that store that Freidman ultimately found his way to The Ticket.

"I let one of my customers run a tab, and I loaned him some money, too," Friedo said. "He was part-time producing a fantasy football show on KLIF, but he ended up getting a full-time job at another station. Somebody at KLIF asked him if he knew anybody who could replace him, and he gave them my name.

"Was it because I was a nice guy? No. It was because I knew sports and he owed me cash," he said. "He didn't get me the job but he got my foot in the door."

Friedman produced the show that aired Sundays from noon to 6 P.M. The irony is that he hates fantasy football, even now. The show consisted mainly of guys calling in and asking questions like, "How many yards did Eddie George get?" "Did he have all-rushing touchdowns, or did he have any receiving scores?" You'd think that the experience would have been torture for Friedo, and soured him on radio forever, but the opposite was the case.

"This was before the Internet was mainstream and before DirecTV and the Sunday Ticket," Friedman said. "This was the only way people could quickly get information about their players. We had correspondents from every NFL stadium giving stats; it was actually a pretty cool show.

"I did that for about a year and decided I really liked radio, and I wanted to continue doing as much as I could, even though I still had the store," he said.

That didn't last too much longer. He and his partner ran the store for a couple more years and then sold it to buy a restaurant in Lewisville. Then they sold that, and Friedman used the money to buy back the convenience store. But, as he puts it, he "ended up getting his ass kicked" financially and wanted to get back into radio full time. Finally, in May of 1993, he landed that full-time gig, producing *The Sports Brothers* and Mike Fisher's show on KLIF.

He was doing everything he could to get hours, even answering the phones at The Ticket after Susquehanna purchased the station.

"I knew I wanted to be at The Ticket, and I knew they wanted me," Friedman said. "There are a lot of people we want here, but no one leaves. Just because they want you here doesn't mean it'll happen. It just happened to work out for me."

It wasn't long before he became producer of Hitzges' show, and then was named assistant program director. His main responsibilities as assistant program director include putting schedules together, hiring part-timers and critiquing the performances of weekend hosts and Ticket Ticker guys.

"Do I ever want to be a program director? Probably not," Friedman said. "That sounds like I'm not ambitious, but I really like the programming, the on-air side of it. Even though I don't like to be on the air, I like to talk to callers—believe it or not, because I act like I don't."

Bread and butter

Friedo has a nice assistant program director title, but where he really makes his dough—and gets his notoriety—is through producing Hitzges' show. If you ever have an HSO you want to share with Norm, you've go to go through Friedo first. So pay attention: you're about to find out what it takes to get past him.

"I still let bad callers on the air; it's not an exact science," Friedman said. "But you can sit here and determine, for the most part, who the good callers are. A 'bad caller' isn't necessarily a person who's not intelligent. But I don't want a caller who says 'I want to know what Norm thinks about the Cowboys.' I want a caller who's going to give his opinion, then see what Norm thinks about that opinion. You don't want a debate all the time, but I also don't want it to be a question-and-answer session."

Friedman pitches in whenever other shows' producers are on vacation or otherwise absent, so he has a good feel for not only Norm's callers, but those of the other shows as well—especially *Dunham & Miller* and *BaD Radio*.

"With Norm, we get a lot of callers who just want to know what he thinks, because he's a sports guru," Friedman said. "With some of the other shows, you'll get people calling in who want to argue with the hosts. When I produce the morning show, some callers want to impress the guys with how funny and creative they are. With Norm, they want to impress him with how much they know about sports. With *BaD Radio*, it's getting to be where they're a lot like The Musers' callers: they're creative, they're funny, and they want to show that."

And other times he gets to experience the other side as a co-host in fill-in shows.

"With some of the fill-in hosts, you get a lot of people calling in who say, 'Tell that jackass he doesn't know what he's talking about,'" Friedman said. "You don't get that with Norm too much; he's been around more than thirty years, and people respect him. That's not to say you don't get people who want to take him on; I like putting on callers like that because it can get explosive.

"But I don't like to be on the air, especially with Norm. It's *The Norm Hitzges Show*, not the Norm and Friedo Show," he added. "A lot of times you'll hear him try to engage me in conversation, and I won't respond. It's not because I'm ignoring him, it's because I don't think the listeners want to hear me. They want to listen to Norm."

Friedman sells himself short, because he does an excellent job on the air, just like The Ticket's Mr. Ticket Ticker himself, Rich Phillips.

Ticker time

Phillips has done so many tickers in his decade-plus at the station, he can effortlessly shift from casual conversation to pitch-perfect presentation. Like his fellow ticker guys Sean Bass, Ty Walker, Mike Sirois and others who do nights and weekends, Phillips is the "hard news" guy every morning on *Dunham & Miller*.

He's got the formula down, to say the least. It usually takes him about five minutes to put together a ticker, which occurs every twenty minutes. His information sources include ESPN.com, WFAA.com (for weather and breaking non-sports news), and the MetroSource newswire service, which provides most of the sound bytes that are intertwined through most tickers. The process of getting that audio is light-years ahead of where it was when he first arrived at The Ticket in 1995; now it's as simple as point-and-click downloading.

The Ticker room is separated from the host's area by another area where the producer and board operator sit. But that doesn't mean Phillips isn't part of the presentation. He can chime in with The Musers just about any time he wants, except during Gordon Keith bits and interviews. And they definitely jack with him; periodically, Gordo will slide in a "Hey, Rich" during a ticker in a vain attempt to throw Phillips off stride.

"I'm a machine by now; that's what happens after twelve and a half years," Phillips said. "[Getting screwed with] used to bother me, but after a while it just doesn't anymore. If I show that I have a problem with it, then I get made to look like the ass on the air. You can't be uptight around here; you have to roll with everything.

"I wonder, if and when I ever move somewhere else, how I'm going to assimilate back into a regular broadcasting environment," he added. "This is a really laid-back place."

A laid-back place with the state-of-the-art equipment befitting a ratings powerhouse. Without attempting a failed effort to accurately describe the functions of all the knobs, dials and buttons that comprise that equipment, suffice it to say that Phillips uses a small operating board in front of him. He used to have to record hundreds of sound bytes a week into a much more primitive system. As stated previously, now all he has to do is find the byte off a computer system that feeds it into the Enco—which, for lack of a better description, is the nerve center of the operation—in a fraction of the time spent before.

It's a far cry from the ancient equipment they used at the Mockingbird Lane studios when Phillips got started with The Ticket. The atmosphere is also a whole lot less tense.

"I never thought we'd be in business this long," Phillips said. "When I came here, it was unstable. We were bought about four months after I got here by Susquehanna, which owned one of our competitors, KLIF. We thought we were finished.

"Dan Bennett assured us that they didn't want to shut us down, but I don't think anybody believed it," he continued. "That was in May of '96. I didn't believe it until June of the next year when they moved us in here. We looked around, saw they had spent all this money on us, then figured they were going to keep us around a while."

Phillips snaps to attention the exact second it comes time for either a ticker tease or the ticker itself. He likens his nearly subconscious reaction to that of Pavlov's dog. But he doesn't have a robotic approach to his job—not having that approach is, in fact, his biggest challenge.

"The toughest thing about this job is trying to be different every day," Phillips said. "I'm a very formulaic person, but I also try to be creative at the same time, not sound like I'm going through the motions."

Someone else who can do his job almost effortlessly is board operator "Big Strong" Jeremy Moran, the glue that keeps the presentation together.

The Drop Masters

Moran and fellow board op Michael "Grubes" Gruber have become Ticket celebrities in their own right. And it goes deeper than the slivers of time they get to actually talk on air. Where they get their notoriety is their uncanny ability to play, or "drop," the right piece of audio at exactly the right moment.

It's hard to describe the talent and lightning-fast thinking it takes to pull this off. When a member of The Musers or *The Hardline* is in mid-sentence, and Moran or Grubes play a drop that is so perfect it makes one of the hosts burst out laughing, that is a true art.

And not everybody has that kind of touch. It isn't something that can be taught.

"Honestly, it's something you either have or you don't," said Moran, who started at The Ticket in August 1997. "A lot of people can run the board fine, but they don't quite get playing drops. Expo [former board op Kevin Fox] and Psycho Dave [former board op Dave Martin] had it. Grubes definitely has it.

"I don't mean to sound cocky, but that's really the way it is," he continued. "There are certain things that keep popping up and you know it's coming, but most of it is instinct."

Again, it would be fruitless to try to accurately paint a picture of the array of computer screens and knobs and dials and other accoutrements that Moran and the other board ops have to twist and tweak. Basically, the Enco Moran uses is the big brother to the one used by the ticker guys. The *really big* big brother. But that equipment, and Moran's, Grubes' and the other board ops' expertise, is what keeps The Ticket broadcasting. Although they do get a little air time, they're mostly just like referees; the less you notice them, the better job they're doing.

Unless they play a golden drop, that is.

"My job is basically to make sure the station sounds OK," Moran said. "Run the commercials at the right time, give the ticker guys the right sponsors and make sure the guys sound good on the air."

As stated about five thousand words ago, the next nine chapters are dedicated to the hosts who make The Ticket what it is. Hopefully you'll get to know each of them a little better, and learn something about each that you never would have imagined was true.

SECTION TWO

The Musers

7

GEORGE DUNHAM

Jub-Jub

"Yeeeeeeeeeaaaaaaaauuuuuuuuuh!"

GEORGE DUNHAM may seem like the quintessential right-winger, The Ticket's bastion of conservatism. While that's true to a certain degree, Dunham is still the same guy who yuks it up daily with fellow Gentle Musers Craig Miller and Gordon Keith, and absolutely tears it up yearly on the Ticketstock stage as a member of the Ticket Timewasters.

"Yeah, I may be a little more liberal than people think," Dunham said. "In my younger years I had my New Wave haircut and I thought U2 was redefining the world. I guess your perspective changes when you have kids.

"I don't really know what the perception of me is," he went on. "Some people think I'm real conservative, while others think I'm a total nut. The opinions are pretty varied, I think. Someone said I'm seen as kind of the normal guy at The Ticket, but if you put me in corporate America I'd probably be seen as the wildest guy in the office."

Whatever the real story is, it started during a childhood that featured three moves as his father was transferred in conjunction with his commercial roofing job. Dunham was born in San Antonio, but he lived in Minneapolis and Chicago before the family returned to Texas.

But it wasn't simply a matter of packing up a kid or two and hitting the road, as Dunham was the youngest of five siblings—all at least ten years older than him.

"I had a great childhood," Dunham said. "My brothers and sisters were always really nice to me. I was the baby of the family, and it was almost like I had another couple of sets of parents because they were so much older. I had a unique relationship with all of them.

"But it was also weird for me, because while I had all these brothers and sisters, it was almost like I was an only child," he said. "By the time I was eight, everyone else was out of the house. From the time I was eight to when I turned eighteen, I was the only child at home."

An unexpected evolution

But unlike his co-host Miller, with whom Dunham has been the best of friends for a quarter century, Dunham didn't grow up dreaming of a career in broadcasting. In fact, it wasn't until he met Junior at the University of North Texas that he even began to entertain the possibility of making a living in radio.

"I listened to a lot of radio growing up, like a lot of kids my age did," Dunham said. "I'd listen to games on my transistor radio, especially when we moved back to Texas when I was in junior high. I used to love to listen to University of Texas games on the old Southwest Conference Radio Network.

"In high school I listened to Brad Sham a lot, and to Norm Hitzges as well," he said. "*The Cowboys Hour, Ask Tex Schramm, The Tom Landry Show*—those shows made my Monday nights because I was such a huge Cowboys fan.

"But I never really thought about doing a talk show for a career," Dunham added. "Craig was a huge influence on me in college. He asked me what my major was, and like a lot of kids I figured I'd get a business degree and maybe go to work for my Dad. I'd have to make a living somehow."

That didn't last long. Miller told Dunham he was pursuing a degree in Radio, Television and Film at UNT, and Dunham thought that it would be a pretty good idea to switch his major to that as well. He and Miller eventually worked at the campus radio station, laying the groundwork for a show that would become a Ticket powerhouse.

"I listened to *CBS Radio Theater*—which was basically a play on the radio—Saturday nights growing up," Dunham said. "We ended up doing some things in college that would eventually find their way to the show."

There happens to be way too much beer to drink and way too many good-looking girls to chase on the North Texas campus. Guys have a lot better things to do than listen to a couple of spares prattle on about sports on the radio. And both Dunham and Miller would probably admit they were exactly that while working at KNTU. So, out of necessity, they would "invent" callers for each other's shows, recording bogus calls in a variety of voices. That way, when the inevitable happened, and the phone lines were dead, they could kill segments.

"I'd have guests and take calls, just like your everyday sports-radio talk show," Dunham said. "The problem was you could only have a guest for so long, and we wouldn't get any calls. I'd ask Craig to give me a guy who wanted to talk about the NT defense, and I'd give him guys with thick country accents talking about whatever Craig needed for his show.

"While we were trying to be legitimate, I don't think we realized at the time that we were introducing the fake elements we use today," he said. "I just became fascinated with the whole idea of radio in college. 'You mean, I could make money doing this?'"

One way to start a career

Dunham started making money in radio straight out of college, working for KRLD in Dallas. Unlike a lot of Ticket hosts, Dunham was fortunate that he didn't have to knock around in a bunch of Podunk towns before hitting a major market. For much of his good fortune, Dunham has fellow UNT grad Craig Way to thank. Dunham basically got to be KRLD's Denton sports correspondent as a result of Way's recommendation. Dunham did high school baseball and football reports for the station, and was hired immediately after he graduated in 1988.

"Anything happened in Denton sports, I would send Craig a tape," Dunham said. "I didn't get paid for it, but it was great. Here I was a college student with no experience and I was on KRLD. It really paid off a couple of years later when I was hired."

When he joined KRLD, Dunham was part of a four-man sports staff that included the aforementioned Sham and Way, as well as

Chuck Cooperstein. He did sports updates on the station for about a year, and while he enjoyed it, he was still the low man on the totem pole, a position which wasn't likely to improve anytime soon. So he jumped at the opportunity to join the Texas State Network, an affiliation of stations throughout the state that was headquartered in the same building as KRLD. Dunham became sports director at TSN while still maintaining a few KRLD responsibilities.

"It was a great opportunity and paid more money, plus I could still do stuff with KRLD when they needed fill-in work," Dunham said. "I could still do the high school game of the week with Craig Way, stuff like that. It was kind of the best of both worlds."

Things were going pretty well for a few years, until TSN started "streamlining" operations, as Dunham put it. In order to keep his job, Dunham realized he'd have to make himself more marketable. So he started getting into the programming and administrative ends of the TSN operation, becoming a "suit" of sorts—his official title was Director of Affiliate Relations—in addition to his sports director duties.

That's what he was doing in the summer of 1993 when Mike Rhyner approached him about jumping on board with a new sports-radio station. Although everyone involved thought he would be the hardest to convince—after all, he was the one with the wife and kids, and therefore would be taking the largest gamble—Dunham immediately agreed to roll the dice.

"It was getting scary at TSN," Dunham said. "I don't know if I had total security, I wasn't making a lot of money, and I wasn't very fulfilled. That's why the whole idea of The Ticket was so appealing. If you were a sportscaster around here in the late eighties and nineties, you had heard of all of these all-sports stations around the country. We knew it would work if somebody tried it here. When Rhynes asked me if I wanted in, I said, 'Heck yeah.' I had some doubts, but I also had great faith it was going to work. It was very clear to me it was the thing to do.

"Sure I had family responsibilities, but again, I wasn't really hesitant because I really thought it would work," Dunham added. "It's

kind of the sports equivalent to coaching: it's like a guy who'd never been any sort of assistant or coordinator being offered a head coaching job. Of course I was going to take it. We may have been getting in way over our heads, but I was willing to see what would happen."

Dunham set aside his minor concerns pretty easily because he was confident that whoever started the first all-sports station in Dallas would succeed, and he wanted to be part of that first effort. But, as detailed in an earlier chapter, the concept of The Ticket was often alive in the morning, dead in the afternoon, then revived in the evening. While Dunham said he wasn't fully aware of that, he had an idea the concept was on some pretty shaky ground.

"We had left our jobs in late October because we thought the station would start in mid-November," Dunham said. "Then the sign-on day was pushed back to December 1 and then December 15. When it was bumped back to January 1, I started to get real nervous.

"But at the same time—not to get overly religious, but I just continued to have the faith that things were going to work somehow," he said. "If it didn't, well, maybe I could have asked for my old job back. But until I heard for sure that The Ticket wasn't going to happen, I wasn't going to seriously consider it."

When The Ticket finally hit the airwaves for the first time in January 1994, it didn't take long for Dunham to realize he had signed on with a winner. "One day that first week me and Craig went to lunch—we didn't go on the air until two—and said, 'Let's listen to Mike and Greg.' It was the day after the Cowboys beat the 49ers to go to the Super Bowl," Dunham said. "I remember Greg saying, 'OK, let's cut the crap' during a segment. I don't even remember what exactly he was talking about, but it was refreshing. I knew nobody else on the air was like us, and off we went."

A bit of a conflict

As much of a winner as The Ticket looked to be in the early days, Dunham had some concerns with just how far "out there" the hosts would go. After all, they were broaching some pretty taboo subjects like no one else in Dallas radio. Comparing the breast sizes of different women at a roadshow was tame compared to some of the other stuff that was making it on air. Dunham, who has made no secret of his strong religious beliefs, bristled on a consistent basis at the—to put it mildly—bawdy tone of much of The Ticket shtick.

"Absolutely I struggled with some of the things we talked about," Dunham said. "It wasn't necessarily a moral question, and it wasn't that I didn't think it belonged on the radio. I looked at it more from how people looked at me as a father, what my kids might say, and what other kids may say to them. I still do.

"I made peace with that, though," he continued. "Just because somebody else may say something on the air, or even if I may say something, even though it may be a little dicey, that doesn't necessarily mean I feel the same way off the air. At the same time, though, it's not necessarily something I'd say around my own child.

"But yeah, it's been a struggle and continues to be one. We are entertainers, and every entertainer at one time or another probably feels weird about that kind of thing."

And then there's Gordo

If Dunham had a problem with the fart jokes, women's genitalia references and the rest of the "dicey" content that made The Ticket stand out, his comfort level had to have been completely obliterated when Gordon Keith became a permanent part of the *Dunham & Miller* show. The Musers had just recently made the move to mornings, and station management thought Gordo would be a better fit in that time slot than in afternoon drive with *The Hardline*.

Keith is portrayed on the show as Dunham's moral opposite, a mild form of nemesis, if you will. Whenever Keith mentions the sex appeal of some gorgeous woman, he'll inevitably turn to the family man and say something like, "You want some of that don't you, Georgio?" He also makes a habit of needling Dunham about his homophobic tendencies. Dunham plays along with Keith's nearly constant badgering, and it makes for great radio. But these exchanges weren't all fun and games in the early days—at least as far as Dunham was concerned.

"I thought Gordo was absolutely hilarious in the limited exposure I had with him at the beginning," Dunham said. "I had heard a couple of bits he had done and thought he was great. But when I started working with him on the morning show he was a real pain in the ass. And he'd admit that.

"You were always on guard with him; you were always waiting for the next Gordo insult. It was never-ending," he went on. "He said some pretty hurtful things on the air and off; you didn't always know how to take it.

"But he's really grown up a lot in fifteen years," Dunham added. "I think he realizes what a jackass he used to be. A lot of people think he still is, but with Gordo it's different. What you hear on the air is totally different from who he is off the air. He's a very private person; he doesn't talk about his family status, and that's fine. But at the same time, you can go to dinner with him and he'll still act like a rambunctious monkey."

Keeping it on track

The Musers have been a morning-drive force ever since they took over the slot in the early days of the station. But even though the show has consistently dominated the ratings, Dunham couldn't even imagine listening to one of their shows from back in the day.

"We were just all over the road," Dunham said. "We didn't have a clear idea of what we wanted to do. For example, we could have said, 'At 8:50 let's talk Cowboys,' and that's all we would have said. Then we would have meandered our way through Cowboys talk. Now it's 'At 8:50, did you hear what Tony Romo had to say? Is that not the most ridiculous thing you've ever heard a quarterback say?'

"That may seem like an elementary thing, but it's amazing," he said. "You go around and listen to sports talk and it's all over the road. 'Hey, the Cowboys played the Giants yesterday. Let us know what you think.' That kind of thing."

Now, Dunham said, the show is not only extremely streamlined, it contains much more "meat," or substance. With each topic, both Dunham and Miller's main concern is whether or not that subject is strong enough to carry a ten-minute segment. "It's sort of like a tree with branches," he said. "Can you build off of it? Whether you're talking about HOV lanes or the Cowboys running game, is there enough meat there? In the old days, it was just kind of like, 'Let's talk Cowboys.' We had good ideas, but they weren't really specific or well thought out."

Has that more streamlined, substance-over-style approach sapped some of the humor out of the show? "I don't know," Dunham said. "In the early days, because we were so free-form, we'd freestyle into something that was just hilarious. We'd never do that now, because we wouldn't want to get off-topic. We don't riff nearly as much as we used to.

"I miss that sometimes," he added, "even though now we riff off of structure. We can still take a topic and riff off of it. Gordon and Craig will still have a funny line, but at the same time we don't wander off."

You again?

George Dunham and Craig Miller have been best friends and nearly daily companions for the better part of a quarter century. But while Dunham has been married with kids nearly all of that time, Miller only recently got married himself. Because of that, the time they spend together after the show has shrunk significantly.

"That's something that's really changed," Dunham said. "We're still really close friends, but we spend so much time together—every morning, five hours together—that we really don't [hang out much] anymore.

"Craig and I just have really different lives. He's married now, and I have my kids," he said. "I do kind of miss that, but it's a way our personal lives have been changed by the show. I don't know if we'd get on each other's nerves if we hung out more, but we just need a natural break."

The two have had their occasional spats, of course, both on and off the air. The staying power of their show is almost unheard of in radio, and it's understandable they'd tear into each other once in a while. After all, it's surprising they've lasted this long, considering they have nearly polar opposite personalities. Miller, Dunham said, is a very organized Type A, while Dunham describes himself as more of a free-flowing spirit.

"We've had several blow-ups, and it's usually from something stupid like who's the better receiver, or whether or not a certain team is overrated," he said. "But it's been a couple of years since we had one because I think we've gotten wiser in that way, too.

"I could start a fight with him tomorrow if I wanted to, but I really don't," Dunham added. "We've kind of learned that about each other over the years. I could really push his buttons, but we don't take shots at each other as much; we've probably worn each other out.

"That may be why he came close to getting burned out. We don't always see eye-to-eye."

Miller did almost quit the show a few years back due to burnout, but Dunham said that was never an option for himself.

"Financially, Craig could give it up, but I'm a provider," Dunham said. "He could go off and do whatever, but I've got to work."

In it for the duration

Just because they may get on each other's nerves every once in a while doesn't mean Dunham and Miller are ready to part ways. And it's not just for financial reasons. Dunham still finds plenty of reasons to get up at the insane hour of 3:45 A.M. every weekday.

"I guess what keeps me coming back is the idea that we're making something out of nothing," Dunham said. "Sometimes I think we have really interesting interviews even if you're not a sports fan. If you're just a human listening, you'd [still] think it was interesting.

"It's also great when we take a sports situation and turn it into something you can laugh at," he said. "That's why the fake characters have always been my favorite part of it; that's that radio theater thing. That's the most rewarding part of it. It goes way back to KNTU twenty years ago and the fake calls."

Asked what his favorite fake character was, Dunham chose Ribby Paultz, the NFL Draft "expert" created by Gordo. "The whole concept was, 'There are all of these draft gurus out there and none of them really say anything worthwhile. Let's come up with our own.' We took a funny concept and Gordon brought it to life."

The constant conundrum

Dunham is always thinking about the show. He's always in mental preparation, whether for the next day's extravaganza or one coming up in a week or a month. In addition to the insane hours he keeps for the show, he does play-by-play for North Texas football and home basketball games, and works as the public address announcer during Cowboys games at Texas Stadium.

"That's the weird thing about what we do: it seems like we're always in mental prep," Dunham said. "It may be something like a stupid billboard I see on the drive home, but I make a mental note or jot it down."

The upside to waking up at 3:45 every weekday morning is that he's there when his kids come home. He can go to their practices or their games and still have enough time to get a decent amount of sleep. It was that way with his son Brent, who's now in college at Arkansas, and his younger sons Blake (who's in high school) and Scott Landry (who's seven).

The downside to his job, and one with which he constantly has to struggle, is how much to expose his family to on-air mentions.

"How much of myself do I share on the air?" Dunham said. "We talk about things in real abstract views, but how much do you really want to say about your own son? Blake started playing Friday night football, and I'd love to talk about him. But at the same time, I respect his privacy. That's *his* Friday night experience. It's his life. I don't in any way want to affect that experience, to have some kid thinking, 'Blake thinks he's all that because his Dad talks about him on the radio.'

"When it's something really near and dear, I don't talk about it too much," he said. "I never really talked about the birth of my sons or experiences like that."

That struggle crystallized in the most painful way one morning in 2004, when his son narrowly escaped death in a boating incident that changed the Dunham family's lives forever.

"Here's a perfect example of why I go back and forth about it," Dunham said. "A few years ago Blake was nearly hit by a boat in the middle of Lake Granbury. We're lake people; we go just about every weekend in the spring and summer. It was a Friday after the show and we all went down there, and we were having a great time.

"Blake was waterskiing behind our boat, and this other guy was recklessly driving another boat," he said. "He was either drunk or a lunatic. Anyway, Blake fell off the skis and the guy was coming right at us. I was turning around to get Blake and I saw the driver and started motioning to him. I slowed down and he veered off and turned right toward my son.

"It was the most terrifying thing, seeing this twenty-two-foot boat going right at my son. I was screaming and jumping up and down," Dunham said. "He finally started turning again, and I thought, 'Thank God,' but then he was about to hit Blake with the back end of his boat. He missed Blake by about three feet.

"It was just horrible. Everybody was crying, and my wife was bawling. I pulled Blake out of the water and had to get my thoughts together," he said. "[The other boater] just kept going; he hauled. I took off to try and catch him or at least get his tag number.

"I haven't looked at life the same way since," Dunham said. "It was last summer before my youngest son could get back in the water. Blake can't really listen to Van Halen because that's what we were playing in the boat. It was very traumatic."

Dunham had a decision to make: how—or if—he would address the near-disaster the following Monday on the show. Would he talk on-air about how this incident changed his life; changed the way he looks at boating, one of his life's passions? Would he approach the topic like he was performing a public service, to say "If you're going to buy a boat, learn how to operate one?" Would he give a description of the boat so somebody could find the bastard?

Like most (if not all) Ticket hosts would have, Dunham decided to open up the entire book and spill all its contents, for better or worse. What followed was one of the most poignant moments in Ticket history.

Sometimes life dictates that you pour out your soul, no matter the consequences.

"I couldn't hold it together on the air. I cried," Dunham said. "After that, there was an e-mail saying unbelievable things, like, 'Yeah, as if it was really that close with your son. We're really supposed to believe that.'

"That's an example of pouring it out on the table and getting negative feedback," he said. "Ninety-nine percent of the listeners understood what I went through. They were great. But that's the one you remember.

"I don't want to come off as the male Oprah, you know, somebody who's trying to make people cry," Dunham added. "But at some point you've got to start talking about life, and those are the things that are most precious to me.

"Again, that's the daily struggle for us....We're almost reality radio, because we bring up so many real-life situations, but how much do you really bring up? How much of yourself are you willing to pour out there and let people kind of pick through the pieces?"

Looking forward

No matter how he still has to confront the issue of how close to let the listener into his personal life, Dunham continues to love his job. And he intends to keep it for many, many years to come.

"Could I see myself doing this for another ten years? Yeah. In fact, I plan on it," Dunham said. "That's a good number to shoot for; that'd get us right to twenty-five years on the air. Wow, that would be a great accomplishment. I think we can. We'll have to re-evaluate it every few years, but yeah, I still hope to be here."

And still with his compadre Craig Miller, who, as you'll find out, made being a sports nerd pay off handsomely.

8

CRAIG MILLER

Junior

"That is *SO* ridiculous."

LIKE MANY of his fellow Ticket hosts, Craig Miller was a little bit of a sports nerd as a kid.

OK, he was a big-time sports nerd. Not that there's anything wrong with that. In Miller's case, it ended up working out pretty well.

Miller was born in Amarillo and moved to New Orleans shortly afterward. When he turned three, the family moved to Oklahoma City and stayed until he was sixteen. Then they moved to Dallas.

"I just remember always loving sports," Miller said. "I don't know what attracted me to it; the same stuff as any kid, I guess. The cool colors in the uniforms, the stadiums—whatever it was, I was obsessed.

"Here's how bad I was. I remember in first grade we had to write something about Christmas," he said. "The teacher took all of the stories, made copies of them, stapled them together, and that was our parents' gift.

"Every kid wrote about Rudolph, Baby Jesus, Santa, the manger scene, whatever—except for me," he said. "I drew a little picture of Roger Staubach and made up a story about him going to the Super Bowl and how the Cowboys won. It had nothing to do with Christmas, but that's how weird I was about sports."

For today, we're looking at a high of...

If not for snapping out of a certain phase when he was seven, Miller today might have been on TV giving you the five-day outlook rather than musing gently every weekday morning from 5:30 to 10 A.M. He was enthralled by the nightly weather broadcast—the maps, the radar, it was all magic to young Junior.

"I decided I wanted to be a TV weatherman," Miller said. "In my closet at home I moved all the clothes to the side and I put maps up and a little fake radar. I put plastic covering over them and did a TV weathercast every night. I'd draw the cold front on there, the temperatures around the state, and did my forecast. It was a great weather center."

Thankfully, that only lasted a year or two before Miller turned his attention back to his first love. He was into sports, so why not go into sports broadcasting? His father took him to several Oklahoma City 89er minor league baseball games, and every time Miller would look down on the field as the local TV sports anchors were doing interviews.

"I thought, 'What a great job. They get to go down there and talk to the players, they get into the game for free, and they get to broadcast about the game,'" Miller said.

By this time he was listening to all the sports he could digest. He kept a small map of the United States in his room by his radio. Every time he was able to pick up a new station from around the country, he'd chart it on the map. (Like you never did anything like that when you were a kid.)

He became a Spurs fan after being able to pick up WOAI-AM out of San Antonio in 1974, when he was nine. It was his first exposure to the American Basketball Association, the league featuring the red, white and blue ball. The ABA lasted only two more years, but the NBA absorbed the Spurs, along with the Indiana Pacers, New Jersey Nets and Denver Nuggets.

"I heard Terry Stembridge, the old voice of the Spurs, doing this San Antonio–Kentucky game. I didn't know anything about the ABA. Nobody knew anything about the ABA in Oklahoma City," Miller said. "I kept listening and it was The Iceman, Louis Dampier and Larry Keenan for the Spurs, and Artis Gilmore for Kentucky. It was a great, exciting game.

"I had stumbled upon a new pro-sports league, and basketball was probably my favorite sport at the time," he said. "San Antonio was a team, and I was born in Texas. I loved Texas. This was really cool."

It is your destiny, Luke...

Miller's discovery of WOAI not only gave him a team to root for, it also provided his first exposure to sports talk radio. In addition to the Denver Pioneer college hockey games he picked up on KOA-AM and the St. Louis Blues games on KMOX-AM, the San Antonio station served up sports talk just about every night.

And Miller was hooked. He listened every night, and called in just about every night as well. (He didn't mention what kind of hell there was to pay from his parents when they received the phone bill.)

Miller's affinity for sports talk radio carried over to his high school days in Dallas, when he and a friend would constantly call shows hosted by Brad Sham on KRLD-AM and Norm Hitzges on WBAP-AM. Of course, since Junior is a well-known smart-ass, he made a slew of prank calls as well. He and a friend named Quinson were in cahoots.

"Every night me and Quinson would prank call Norm or Brad," Miller said. "Brad was tougher because he had a seven-second delay on KRLD. Norm on WBAP didn't have any delay, so we could prank him any night. Norm didn't have many callers, so he welcomed us; he put us on the air all the time.

"I remember he had the trainer for the Rangers on one night," Miller said. "Quinson called in and said, 'Yeah, I've got two questions. Number one; what kind of program do you have Buddy Bell on? And number two, do you recommend a stringent weight training program for billiards?'

"Norm told the trainer, 'Now that's Quinson, and that's a fooler question. But you can answer the first one.'"

Junior and Quinson thought they had received their first break when they found out Norm was leaving WBAP. His temporary replacement, Dr. Dan Flanagan, made it known to listeners that he didn't plan on making the talk show his full-time gig, and sent out an open request for résumé tapes on the air. They were taking them from anybody, so the two youngsters decided to seize the day.

"Q and I snuck out of school at eleven in the morning, made a horrible résumé tape and waited for Dr. Flanagan in the parking lot," Miller said. "When he came out we gave him the résumé tape and applied for Norm's job—as seniors in high school.

"For some reason, we didn't get the job."

Hello, George

Undeterred by the WBAP rejection, Miller enrolled at North Texas State (now the University of North Texas) in the fall of 1983. On his second day of freshman English, Miller would meet George Dunham, the person with whom he's been joined at the hip for more than twenty-five years.

"I didn't know him at all," Miller said. "On Wednesday he sat down beside me because, he said, my side of the room was funnier. Me and a couple of other guys had been joking around on Monday."

Simple as that. Soon Dunham and Miller discovered they were living in the same dorm, and Dunham would soon move across the hall. Miller said there was no particular conversation he could recall that made he and Dunham hit it off. There was the obvious shared love of sports, and the fact that they shared an off-beat sense of humor. But what probably formed their strongest bond was the

fact they were both huge fans of then-Cowboys quarterback Danny White.

"We took that and ran with it," Miller said. "We found out when the other would have a class in another building, and would wait until that class was halfway through. I would open the door to that class and walk in pretending I was going into the right room, and I was also pretending I was having a conversation.

"The professor would be in the middle of a lecture and I'd walk in and say, 'Yeah, that's right. As I recall, I was thinking it was Danny White,'" he said. "We'd do stupid stuff like that all the time."

Dunham originally planned on being a business major, but changed his plan at Miller's urging to Radio, Television and Film. "I kind of talked him into it," Miller said. "I told him, 'It's fun, it's sports broadcasting, and you only have to take three hours of math. It's a pretty easy degree.'"

The two worked at the campus radio station until graduation, then parted ways for a short time. Miller was doing an internship at KDFW-TV, while Dunham was able to immediately get a job at KRLD-AM. Miller was paying the bills by also working at a new jazz station in Denton, KJZY-FM.

For a little while, at least.

"I got fired after three weeks," Miller said. "The program director didn't like the way I was personalizing my presentation—I was doing sports mainly, but on the weekends I had a DJ shift. 'All you have to do,' he said, 'is play the records. You're adding too much, trying to be funny.'

"He also said he didn't like some of the music I was playing. 'We need upbeat music,' he said. So I hung up the phone and found the longest, most depressing, slowest jazz song I could find. It was about twenty-five minutes long. He called me back and told me not to worry about coming to work anymore."

Breaking away

Miller started looking around for a TV job, but the best offer he received was doing the early morning farm report on a station in Ada, Oklahoma for $4.50 an hour. Hit hard by the lack of anything close to resembling a quality prospect, Miller started worrying whether or not he'd ever be able to find a job in broadcasting, and started wondering whether the four years he had spent at North Texas had been a colossal waste of time.

Sometimes, when faced with such a bleak outlook, the best thing to do is get the hell out of Dodge. And that's what Junior did. An old friend of Miller's convinced him to take a year off from the job search and move to Colorado. Miller and his friend were bike racing fanatics, and at that time Colorado was a bicycling Mecca. They figured they'd train every day, enter as many races as they could, and get bartending jobs to pay the bills. Miller had a girlfriend at the time in Dallas so the decision was a difficult one, but he decided to make the move.

"We had dated for two or three years, but the relationship was wobbling a little bit, and she knew this was something I really wanted to do," Miller said. "It was really tough; I remember leaving her that morning and we were both bawling. But we agreed that we'd each other every month; either she'd fly to Colorado or I'd fly down to Dallas. We were able to stay together the whole time, but maybe subconsciously we could both see the writing on the wall.

Despite this, he said, "I had a blast in Colorado. I won my third race, so I thought I was the next Greg LeMond. I said, 'Forget broadcasting, I'm going to be a professional bike racer. Well, I didn't win another race the rest of the year. Reality sunk in pretty quick that you have to be extra special to succeed at any sport professionally, and I wasn't extra special."

It would be a sappy overstatement to say that Miller went to Colorado to "find himself," but a visit to a Boulder bookstore made him realize he needed to get back to Dallas. "I still knew I wanted to get into broadcasting," Miller said. "I was in the bookstore one day and picked up a sports almanac, and the sports bug bit me again. I missed it, and I knew it was where I wanted to be."

The year was coming to a close, so Miller called his old friend Dunham and asked what sort of gigs might be available. It just so happened one of the reporters at KRLD was leaving for San Antonio, and Dunham had told Brad Sham about Miller. Sham was interested, so Miller sent him a demo tape and résumé.

"[Sham] had a history of hiring guys from the University of North Texas, and he trusted George," Miller said. "So I went and got a newspaper, cut it up, pasted some stories together, wrote a little sportscast and 'broadcast' it into a hand-held tape recorder. I FedExed the tape and résumé to Brad, and a couple of days later he called. I had a thirty-minute interview over the phone, and he asked me when I could start."

Helloooo...Anybody out there?

It was the fall of 1990 when Miller started at KRLD. He started off doing evening and weekend sportscasts, and weekend sports talk shows called *Sports Central Saturday* and *Sports Central Sunday*. He also covered games, getting sound bytes on tape. Then he'd take those tapes back to the station so that the morning host, Chuck Cooperstein, could use them on the air.

But this was a time when KRLD was faltering. Severely. The station had lost rights to broadcast Dallas Cowboys games, and the resulting effects were crippling. Soon the station was forced to fire a third of its staff. Miller kept his job, but his hours were cut back. He made up time by operating the board for overnight shows, while still working his usual sports shift during the week. So he'd work from 5 to 11 P.M. doing sportscasts, then from midnight to 6 A.M. on the board.

Eventually he was able to grab the afternoon shift doing sports for the Texas State Network, which had an affiliate in every city and town in the state. KRLD was the Dallas affiliate, so Miller was able to continue his KRLD duties and work at TSN at the same time.

The TSN show was a disaster. Because most affiliates around the state chose—understandably, of course—to broadcast Spurs, Rangers, Astros or Mavericks games, depending on what section of the state they were in, it was rare that a station would carry Miller's talk show.

Which meant that nobody was listening. Nobody was calling in. It got so bad that Miller begged all his friends to call the show. George would call in, often multiple times a night, each time using a different voice.

"I called my friends and said, 'Man, I'm dying here. Please call in and ask me questions. I'll keep you on the air for twenty minutes if you want; I don't care,'" Miller said. "George and I used to do the same thing in college. We had a talk show once a week, and whichever one of us didn't host would leave three fake calls on tape. I don't remember George's fake names, but he did three voices. One would be a country guy, the other would be a black guy, and the other would be whatever.

"I had two hours to kill, so I just read out of the newspaper and begged for calls," he said. "I'm telling you, it made me think that if I could just talk for two hours, I could do anything. I didn't have anybody to talk to, nobody to bounce things off of; I was my own board op. Doing a show with somebody else? How easy would that be?

"I remember getting one or two legitimate calls, and both of them were from the board op of an affiliate in El Campo," Miller added. "He had to be the only guy listening."

A new lease on life

Those lonely nights in the TSN studio must have created the same kind of doubt in Miller's mind that he had experienced soon after graduating college. Nothing was on the horizon. He was the low man on the totem pole at TSN and KRLD, and he wasn't moving up anytime soon. But if there were doubts, Miller didn't dwell on it.

"I had a few 'What the hell am I doing?' kinds of moments sitting there, but I never thought this wasn't going anywhere," Miller said. "I always thought it was going somewhere. I was at least putting something on my résumé. I was working on a talk show, even if nobody was listening. I never thought I'd do a talk show the rest of my life. Jobs were few and far between, but I still thought I could do play-by-play, maybe TV sportscasting, something like that. Or just radio sportscasts. Maybe I could find a job in a different market doing morning drive…"

The story of how Miller came to The Ticket has already been covered, but the uncertainty of the early days wasn't limited to whether or not the station would survive from one day to the next. The original plan was for Miller to partner with Mike Rhyner and Greg Williams in an afternoon show that would do battle with Dallas-Fort Worth sports radio stalwart Randy Galloway on WBAP.

"I thought the idea was great, but Rhyner and Williams were two pretty powerful personalities," Miller said. "I thought I might get lost in the mix.

"The more I thought about it, the more it made sense for me and George to do a show, and for Mike and Greg to do a show," he said. "I approached George and he was all for it. He was excited about the potential, about what The Ticket could become."

Rhyner agreed, and Miller and Dunham were once again a team.

They started out in the odd time slot of 2–5 P.M., which lasted for a year and a half. In October of 1995, The Musers moved to the 5:30–10 A.M. shift, where they've thrived ever since.

Up and at 'em

The hours are definitely brutal—Miller wakes up every weekday around three or four in the morning to prep for his show—but the adjustment wasn't that difficult for him. He had previous experience working overnight at KRLD, and had held plenty of jobs waiting tables during college, which kept him up well into the night. So functioning at an odd hour really isn't a problem.

But his ability to get after it the second he wakes up almost makes you want to throw up.

"When we moved to mornings, I absolutely loved it," Miller said. "I'm the kind of guy that when the alarm goes off I'm at full speed. I don't have to hit the snooze; I'm not groggy for twenty or thirty minutes. Guys make fun of me on road trips; Gordo says that when the alarm goes off, a minute later I'm fully clothed with my briefcase, ready to go.

He's very happy about his current schedule. "I'll eat immediately after the show, take a one or two hour nap, then ride my bike or run, eat dinner and watch a game. I'm usually in bed by nine or ten."

Not that he didn't have to learn the hard way just how that shift can cripple your social life—at least during the week.

"It wasn't that bad when I was single, because I could still stay up late Friday and Saturday nights," Miller said. "But one of the first nights after we moved to mornings, Gordo and I went to a happy hour on a Wednesday night. We were plastered by nine.

"The alarm went off the next morning, and I was still drunk," he said. "I came into work and opened the sports page and couldn't focus on the words because I was still hammered. I thought, 'My God, I'm going to have to take a sick day because I'm drunk. I can't go on the air because I'm going to slur my words.'

"I thought, 'Even though I'm not a coffee drinker, I'm going to pound coffee and let George do all the talking until I feel sober," Miller added. "That lasted for about forty-five minutes. I don't think I've been drunk since on a work night. I learned my lesson."

Speaking of him being a single guy, Miller held tightly to his bachelor lifestyle until he was nearly forty. But he finally met the right girl, Aimee, and decided it was time to pull the trigger. "I never thought I'd get married. I never said to myself that I wouldn't, but I loved being single," Miller said. "There was no pressure, nobody to answer to. Any girl I had dated, I couldn't picture myself living with them forever.

"But with Aimee, everything clicked from the beginning," he said. "She was the first girl who didn't make a big deal out of little things. I think that's the key to marriage. I thought I could live with her forever."

Back to the show

For the most part, Miller likes the way the show has evolved. He refuses to listen to tapes from the early days or even today. "I don't like listening to our show anyway," he said, "because I hate my voice, and I think I suck." He thinks the show was awful when it first started but says it's come a long way.

"I think we do a pretty good show," Miller said, "because we've found a balance and a comfort zone. In the early days we tried to be all sports; if we had stayed on that path, we wouldn't [still] be around. But at the same time, you can't do too much screwing around. We're much more at ease with who we are, with our strengths and limitations.

"In the early days we were affected by what everybody else thought, especially our peers," he said. "Now we don't care—we care in that we love constructive feedback, but we let go of a lot of the early criticism. Once we did that, we didn't worry about what our family, the people at church or the guys at the game would think about what we said. When we started going with our natural feelings about a topic, I think the show got a lot better."

But it hasn't been all fun and yuks. A couple of years ago Miller said he seriously considered leaving the show. "I was burned out. *Really* burned out. I almost felt I was at the end of the rope, and I didn't know if I could sign another deal here.

"I just got tired of having to have hot sports opinions every day and then getting barbecued for half of them," he said. "Part of the problem was e-mail. I was answering them all the time; I got bombarded, and I got tired of arguing. That led to me getting tired of arguing sports on the air. One of the ways I cured that was I stopped answering my e-mail.

"George and Gordo probably knew about it, because I got a little testy from time to time," Miller added. "But I think in the end I worked through it."

And he must have, because Miller and Dunham signed a five-year contract with The Ticket in 2007. Can Miller see himself being at The Ticket for its twentieth or twenty-fifth anniversaries? "I could see myself being around for ten years, but I'd like to live in the mountains one day," he said. "I don't know that it has to be in five, ten or fifteen years, but I want to live somewhere really cool before I get too old to enjoy it.

"You know, there are so many variables," he said. "I could easily see myself being here in ten years, because I think George, Gordo and I get along well enough that we can keep this thing going, but it's an impossible question to answer. If the audience gets tired of us and ratings drop, will The Ticket want to keep us? Am I going to have kids? If so, then I'll probably have to work longer than I think."

If so, hopefully he'll still be working with Dunham and Gordon Keith, The Ticket's most intriguing—and possibly funniest—personality.

9

GORDON KEITH
The Great Gordo

"He's the poster boy for underachievement."

GORDON KEITH is probably the most complex personality on The Ticket. He's The Ticket's "X factor": the ingredient that set the station far apart from what most would associate with the term "sports radio." In fact, Keith probably set the station *too* far apart from that mold for most of The Ticket bigwigs' tastes in the early days, but he has unquestionably been one of the driving forces in creating the special niche the station enjoys.

If Keith had any dreams growing up, they sure didn't involve being part of a morning-drive radio talk show. First he wanted to be a doctor, then he envisioned himself as kind of a Renaissance man. His childhood was shaped by several moves, one of which had a very profound effect on him.

Movin' on

"My father was a pastor, so we moved every year and a half when I was very young," Keith said. "Those early moves didn't affect me as much as the later ones, particularly the one during first grade to the Gulf coast, and then the big one in seventh grade when I moved to Dallas.

"Those moves were very traumatic for me," he said. "I lost a certain sense of safety, and part of me goes back to those places often. But I try to comfort myself, knowing that many good things came from those dislocations. If I hadn't moved to Dallas, I would not have met certain special people in my life, and I would not have fallen into the career that I have.

"When I was in elementary school I wanted to be a doctor. Then, as I got into junior high and high school, I began to have vague plans of being some sort of creative type, in print or TV, I didn't know," Keith said. "Then in college, I was just overwhelmed that I had to choose *something*. You know, life demands a response, and you have everyone at every turn pushing you to define yourself. I could never quite get over the fact that you couldn't have multiple lives with multiple passions. I suppose that's why every multi-purpose man from da Vinci to Steve Martin has appealed to me. A man who could live multiple lives in one."

Keith found out about The Ticket from a classmate who knew Mike Rhyner. He applied for an internship shortly before the station went on the air, and within weeks he was on the air himself, doing bits for Skip Bayless' morning show. But that didn't last long, and he was relegated to bouncing around the nether regions, the wasteland of The Ticket: nights and weekends. He was on the long-lost *Late Night Ticket*, then started *The Rant* in 1997, which originally aired at midnight on Saturdays.

Keith started the latter as a lark, he said. When he was bored he'd sometimes go to the station late at night on the weekends while it was airing Sporting News Radio network programming. He'd just turn on the microphone and started doing a show. Sometimes, he said, he'd go until 4 A.M. if he had enough callers who were good and drunk. He'd do the "show" until he got tired of it, then return The Ticket to network programming.

The Rant eventually moved to Saturday mornings and became a kind of farm system for The Ticket weekday big leagues. Several people, like Corby, Gen X Davey and Big Strong Jeremy cut their chops on *The Rant*. "*The Rant* was a great experiment in radio for us," Keith said. "We brought a lot of little *Rant* tricks to the weekday shows and I think made our crazy-head stuff viral.

"In the very beginning, though, I did some call-in characters for Skip Bayless, but Skip and comedy are like oil and water," he said. "He got me off of that show after about a month. Then I bumped around for a while, then I started doing bits for *The Hardline* and The Musers when both of those shows were in the mid-days.

"That was a really fun time—hanging out with *The Hardline* and Dunham and Miller and just going on the air whenever we had an idea," he said. "We were the 'filler' part of the line-up, so we had little fear of experimentation. Now, if we experiment and fail, it's more damaging. With success comes a much higher bar, although you couldn't tell that by listening to us.

"It is always a fine dance to get the right balance between giving the listener something he expects and surprising him, too," Keith said. "You have got to reinvent all the time, but also stay the same product people have come to desire."

Almost a short stay

Keith almost didn't get the chance to reinvent himself at all, because his neck was on the chopping block quite a few times in the early years. He had never planned to be in radio, much less in sports radio, much *much* less in AM sports radio. All he wanted was to maybe get a couple of months out of it, just to say he'd had the experience, and then get on with another adventure.

"My first year I think I made something like $7,900. And from what I understand, when it came time to trim fat out of the budget, our owner said, 'Well, we could do two things: get rid of Gordon or reduce office supplies,'" Keith said. "I'm not sure who went to bat for me, but someone did, and I stayed on after we cut office supplies by an extra 15 percent.

"It wasn't until The Laddy came on board that I really gained some legitimacy," he said. "Until then, I was an odd accessory to the radio station, a sort of 'Gordon, the cubicle guy.' Then The Laddy came along and said, 'This is someone we can really use.'

"So he moved George, Craig and myself to morning drive and *The Hardline* to evening drive. Until him, those two shows were seen as expendable, and he rightly recognized that George and Craig and Mike and Greg were the stars. Those were the shows that the P1s would really talk about, that they connected with. I was just glad to be a part of their world."

Keith's bits grew in number and importance to the station. His appearances around town in a devil suit became legendary, as did his arrest in Green Bay after being accused of trying to deface the "G" on the fifty-yard-line at Lambeau Field.

"People still come up to me to talk about the Lambeau Field ar-

Greggo, Rhyner, Gordo and Cat the night before the Devil's Own would be detained by the police at Lambeau Field.

rest. Only time in my life I have been arrested," Keith said. "It was such a bum rap. I had some security woman's permission to enter the stadium, but I guess I didn't have permission to run around on the field while broadcasting on a cell phone and yelling Packer insults. The cop was pretty rough with me, although I didn't resist.

"For three hours, I sat in a jail cell with a young kid named Quincy (not Carter) who was arrested for crack and assault," he said. "I tried to organize a soccer team with him to break out, but *The Hardline* posted bail before we could choose positions."

Keith doesn't talk a lot about his all-time favorite bits, but he does say there are a couple at the top of his list.

"I think the old Ken Hitchcock/Microphone Johnson interview was a classic," Keith said. "I also remember being proud of the 'Spare Wars' bit. I liked the writing, and I loved the fact that I got to do so many voices in it. It was kind of like living my Mel Blanc dream, I suppose. And although the age has passed, the character I have always enjoyed doing the most is Fake Greggo. There is just such fantastic, crazy range to that character. He can be cocky, stupid, lovable, manic, country, boyish, metropolitan and pithy, all in one bit. The character that I get asked the most to do is Fake Jerry. I don't know why, because I don't even think it sounds like him, but I have left a lot of requested messages on people's answering machines as Fake Jerry.

"To be quite honest, I have a very poor memory about our on-air stuff," he said. "I pretty much forget everything right after we do it. At ten o'clock, I'm off to a different life altogether."

His irreverence and complete and utter lack of knowledge about— or even interest in—sports endeared him, ironically, to listeners who tuned in to hear sports talk. That lack of interest in athletics, he said, actually helped him become accepted by most of The Ticket hosts. He played no small role in taking the station away from the sports page exclusively and more into the realm of "guy talk."

"It maybe hurt me with the Chuck Cooperstein–types, but I wasn't any threat to any of those guys because I couldn't do what they did," Keith said. "I also think that my lack of sports knowledge had a very unintentional positive impact on the station.

"When I started at The Ticket it was a very Xs and Os station, so the only way I could even create a job for myself was by bringing my humor to that equation," he said. "I remember George Dunham once said very early on that The Ticket's secret weapon was me. That was very flattering to me as a directionless young man. Here I was around all these really incredibly talented broadcasters, and this man said *I* was a secret weapon? Made me nervous for their futures.

"But I think his point was that, in those days, I was one of the things that differentiated us from old-time sports radio, [my] stupid characters and stuff," Keith went on. "George, Craig, Mike and Greg are all incredibly funny and witty people, and I always liked it best when they were goofing around. So my job, as I saw it in those days, was to get them to goof around as much as possible, not because I thought it was a grand plan to reinvent sports radio, but because that was the only way I could tolerate listening to the station. I just wanted to hear them like I heard them off the air, laughing hard and being goofy. And that is what ultimately made The Ticket so successful—the stellar personalities of those original guys."

Time to grow up

Keith did eventually grow disenchanted with his aggression-fueled humor of the early years.

"I think I suffered from what many of us have suffered from—the jackassery of youth," he said. "I think I was more aggressive and had not grown the virtue of compassion, which I now see at the core of any decent human being. It is still hard to execute the job I am hired to do and show compassion. I am frequently conflicted, and I often fail to do the right thing.

"I think The Ticket has had a tremendous effect on my maturation. Success can make some a monster, but for me it took the monster away. The Ticket's success brought me a tremendous sense of gratitude and peace," he said. "Unfortunately, I had to grow up in front of people. Most people get the chance to grow up out of the public eye, and then get to start somewhere fresh every few years, but I'm at the same job I have had since college, and some memories are long and unforgiving.

"One of the most gracious things you can do for a man is forgive him his youth. And I hope that people will forgive me mine and show me some mercy as I feel my way through the world like everybody else. Can we get back to Fake Jerry now?"

Keith has not only matured personally, he has also refined his on-air presentation, just as all the other hosts have. He doesn't look back on his early days with disdain like Craig Miller does, but he knows he does a much better job now. He finds his old bits, some of which lasted up to fifteen minutes, lacking in fundamentals. Good bits need punch lines and brevity, and they had neither back then.

"If you have a decent story, some interesting conflict and five good jokes," he said, "then you have a good, solid formula for a funny bit. I think now we have gotten good at making a consistent,

sellable and compelling product. We use our time much more effectively on the air than we did in the early days when we were still
trying out different rudders. The idea is that a listener can tune
in for twenty minutes and hear a complete show—funny, serious,
some sports, some life topic, and then maybe do a bit.

"My role is still the same—to provide the sizzle to their steak,
to kind of safety-dance about the periphery, throwing in lines here
and there and hanging back when they have to get meaty," he said.
"Our show is very intentional. We try to checkerboard sports segments and non-sports segments. Every twenty minutes, we try
to give the blend that people have in their own lives. This is all
behind-the-scenes stuff, and if we are doing our jobs properly, we
conceal the artistry and just show 'em the baby. I think I mixed
about three different metaphors there. Hey, I never claimed to be
smart."

Although one of Gordon Keith's trademarks is making George
Dunham uncomfortable, Keith insists he gets along well with his
fellow Musers both on and off the air.

"The three of us are very close. We share an experience that can't
really be transplanted to anyone else," Keith said. "There are certain psychological difficulties that come with a job such as this, and
there are two people who share my experience so precisely that it
strengthens our bond.

"It's a little like being in a band. Speaking of bands, I remember
some wisdom from the best. Not that I'm comparing ourselves to
them in the least, but I remember George Martin once said about
the Beatles something like, 'Only those four know what it was like
to be in the middle of that storm.' I think there are only a handful of
people at The Ticket who understand what it is like to have been in
the middle of this little Ticket storm from the beginning, and even
those of us who have been buffeted about by it all these years don't
really understand it very well. So at some point you just learn to
shut up and enjoy the small ride God has provided for you.

"Great, now I sound all sappy and sickening. Let me cuss a little
to deflate this. Hell, damn, bottom!"

His face is all over the place

In a way, Keith has become that multifaceted renaissance man he wanted to be growing up. In addition to his work on The Ticket, he writes a weekly column for *Quick*, a publication of *The Dallas Morning News* and has *The Gordon Keith Show* on WFAA-TV (Channel 8). But his natural inclination toward laziness nearly led him to decline that offer.

"About three years ago, the GM of Channel 8 approached me and asked if I would meet her about doing a TV show," Keith said. "She was aware of my writing in *Quick*, and of course knew The Ticket because her ex-husband was a big P1. He had apparently been campaigning for years for her to give me a job.

"So I met with her and a guy named Mike Devlin who is now the GM of WFAA. They wanted me to do a show and it was pretty much *tabula rasa*. I kind of hemmed and hawed and at one point was ready to turn them down, which looking back on it now seems crazy," he said. "How often does someone just offer you such a good opportunity? But my reasons for turning down the opportunity were horrible. I had a fear of failure because I knew I was going to play a different character on the TV thing than I was doing on radio. Plus, TV is a lot of work that you don't see, and I really didn't *need* the extra time commitment. So here I am thinking, 'Hey, WFAA, one of the best-known stations in the country, is wanting to give me a show, and here I am thinking of turning them down out of fear of failure and laziness? That ain't good.'

"Then I imagined a son coming to me someday and saying, 'Dad, I have this great opportunity for a really great job, but I don't want to do it because I am scared of failing, and I am being lazy.' What advice would I give him?" Keith continued. "Well, it was obvious what I would tell him, so shouldn't I be willing to live the advice? So I called them and told them yes.

"They wanted to sign a year deal, and I was so scared of the time commitment, I would only sign a twelve-week deal," he said. "Now that twelve weeks is more than a year and half, and I am very proud of our accomplishment. We could be canceled tomorrow, and probably will be, but my goal was to make it through that first twelve weeks. I always thought that if we could survive beyond that, it [would be] a real gift to add to my catalogue of experiences.

"It has been the biggest growth experience I have ever endured. I proved to myself that I could wade into that horrible maw of public critique and schadenfreude and come out the other side still alive. It reminds me of when I first started my work at The Ticket, or first started the column. It takes awhile for people to accept you."

"Schadenfreude"? Told you the guy's complex.

"Some people tune into the TV wanting The Ticket, but that can't happen," Keith said. It is a different product entirely, and I should have chosen a different name to go by on TV so people wouldn't expect the same character they hear on The Ticket. Telly Beardman, maybe?

Hosting a TV talk show, Keith said, like hosting a radio show, is an incredibly difficult job to do successfully. The TV host has to play every sitcom character and archetype at the same time. You have to be the straight man, the smartass, the clock manager, the content manager, the boy next door, the lovable young man, the upstart, the physical actor, the listener, the reactor, the fire starter, the fireman and the easygoing sidekick—all at the same time you're carrying on a conversation, thinking two minutes ahead, getting the blocking right. It's like flying a plane while juggling to entertain people who are throwing tomatoes at you. And you're supposed to look like you're doing none of it!

"At least on the radio we have different guys to play the different parts; with TV hosting you are all alone," Keith said. "You can't underestimate how hard it is to do a show with no one to bounce off of."

And although he has his own TV show, Keith refutes the perception that he'd love to be a cast member of *Saturday Night Live*.

"I don't know why this *SNL* thing keeps coming up," Keith said. "There used to be this rumor floating around that I tried out for it.

That's totally untrue, but funny. *SNL* cast member is a tremendously difficult job, and not one I desire. Those guys have real talent. I'm just lucky.

"I wanted to do a little bit of everything, but I'm glad talk radio came to me," he said. "I love the intimacy of talk radio. There is something about that voice so close to the microphone that it approximates pillow talk. You don't have that in TV, where the viewer can see the distance. With radio that distance collapses; it's no wonder that some people feel as close to these disembodied voices as they do to their relatives. You spend that many hours a week listening to somebody that intimately, no wonder you forget it's a show."

Keith is an extremely private person. And that's pretty tough to be when you're a very significant celebrity in Dallas. It's his prerogative to be that way, of course, but it's also a curiosity.

"My take on it is that my family has done nothing to deserve the scrutiny that I grew up with and continue to experience," Keith said. "After the first 'I hope your kid gets cancer after what you said about the Rangers' type of e-mail, I realized there was no need to bring my family into my line of fire.

"Everyone has a different level of squeamishness about his privacy or lack thereof, and for some reason I was born with a greater defect than most," he said. "I wish I was comfortable living in a diorama, and having my family there with me, but I'm not. I like going and performing my part and then going back home to a small, simple world. I grew up in small towns, and I guess I am still there in many ways.

"Some people like to say, 'You knew that this was part of the job when you took it,'" Keith said. "The hell I did! Man, I was a dumb kid in junior college who had no idea that my career would go this way. And yes, I could quit all my jobs, but I am really unskilled at anything else. Once you got a bunch of bills, you gotta pay them."

And he's not overly concerned with misperceptions some may have of him.

"To correct certain misperceptions probably only creates more, so why start?" Keith said. "I will say this; my current job is to portray a certain character on the air. Some might confuse the persona with the person."

Not going Hollywood

So will Keith ever follow the siren song of television and try to go national? That's not likely, as he says he plans on being around for The Ticket's twentieth, and maybe even twenty-fifth anniversaries.

"I know plans can change, but I sure hope I'm doing The Ticket in ten years," Keith said. "It has been a wonderful job that has brought me many great blessings and friendships. I love my teammates. It is a rewarding job. I used to downplay the importance of entertainment. We don't cure cancer, but maybe we can keep the guy who ends up curing cancer happy and less burned out on his way in to work. That is worth something.

"I have heard many touching stories from P1s about how much a little radio station can mean to a person," he said. "There was a guy who came up to me with tears in his eyes who told me how much his wife loved listening to The Ticket as he held her hand for dialysis. He said she fought hard.

"There was another guy who told me that the only commonality that he had found to melt the icy relationship with his dad was The Ticket, and how our 'dad talk' provided an entrée for a middle-aged man to finally gain a father," he said. "Stuff like that means something. We are just a small part of the mysterious ways in which God works. Why resist that?

"The Ticket is a really special place, and I think we were all incredibly lucky to have jumped on a train that was actually going somewhere. I try not to deconstruct it too much, because ultimately, unexamined magic is the only kind there is."

SECTION THREE

The Dallas Radio Legend

10

NORM HITZGES

Norm(!)

"Do you know what the hell I do for a living?"

I T'S A CLICHÉ FOR SURE, but Norm Hitzges has definitely seen it all in a broadcasting career that is nearing the forty-year mark. He's interviewed the biggest names in sports, made thousands of friends and been inducted into the Texas Radio Hall of Fame.

He's also been given last rites after a car wreck, lived homeless on a Texas beach, survived incredibly dangerous spinal surgery and traveled across the world.

You could say the guy has led a pretty full life.

Hitzges was born in 1944 in Dunkirk, New York, a little town on Lake Erie about thirty-five miles southwest of Buffalo. His family had no money; his father Edgar never earned more than $250 a week in his life, and his mother Lillian worked in a laundry six days a week for $1 an hour. Edgar lost his job as a machinist at Niagara Motors when the owner shut down the plant after a six-month strike. The rotting building remains standing today.

"We were very poor, but I didn't know it," Hitzges said. "I had a great childhood."

He worked some odd jobs when he was in high school. He dug construction ditches and took over his dad's bartending job for a few weeks one summer while his father was recuperating from a broken ankle. Hitzges got his first journalism job at the *Dunkirk Evening Observer*, proofreading and reporting.

Then he earned an academic scholarship to Canisius College in Buffalo, a place he still cherishes.

"I loved that school," Hitzges said. "It was run by Jesuit fathers, and they dedicated their lives to teaching. I got a better education there than I could have ever dreamed of."

Hitzges even got the chance to play college basketball—even if it was for only three games. He was assistant trainer for the team, and when most of the players flunked out his freshman year, he got to see a little action. But that was the beginning and end of his college basketball career.

Headed to Texas

Every student at Canisius was required to meet with a counselor once every semester. The first semester of his senior year, Hitzges met with Father Murray, an eighty-something priest who helped Hitzges on the road to Texas.

"He asked me where I was planning to go for graduate school, and I told him I was thinking about either Syracuse or Columbia," Hitzges said. "Father Murray would always look up as he was addressing you, like he was looking at something over your shoulder. He said, 'No, no . . . I would not do that. Were I a young man again, I'd go some place I've never been.'

"I thought, 'Well, he's losing it,'" Hitzges said. "I left my meeting with him, walked down the hall, walked outside, and there was about a foot and a half of snow on the ground. Then I said to myself, 'Maybe Father Murray's not losing it. I need to go someplace warm.' I got in touch with three or four schools, and Texas offered me a graduate assistantship to go down there, so I went."

Hitzges hadn't thought much about a broadcasting career, but he did want to write about sports. The *Dunkirk Evening Observer* offered him their sports editor position, but he decided he wanted to pursue graduate study more. He was a combination English/philosophy major at Canisius because the school didn't offer a journalism course. Texas did, so he became a journalism major there.

He stayed at Texas for a couple of years before deciding to put his graduate work on hold and get a job. Hitzges landed at Sul Ross State University. What he didn't realize was that he had stepped into a sweatshop; Hitzges was not only a journalism teacher, he was responsible for putting together the school yearbook, was the school's sports information director and did play-by-play for football and basketball games. All for about $7,500 a year.

"It was a ridiculous job, plus the school had a rule that I couldn't date any students," Hitzges said. "I was twenty-three at the time, and that didn't work for me at all."

Norm has a captive audience in Junior and Corby at a GNO roundtable.

Hitzges moved on to teach high school in San Antonio for a couple of years. He also tried out two years in a row for the San Antonio Toros' semi-pro football team. Hitzges was a kicker in high school and thought he'd take a shot at the same position for the Toros, but a broken ankle suffered in a scrimmage scrum iced those ideas for good.

Life-changing experience

Hitzges was just getting over the broken ankle and heading back to Austin to continue graduate school when a car wreck shattered his body and nearly cost him his life.

It was the fall of 1970 and he was traveling north on rain-slick Interstate 35 outside of San Marcos. A woman headed in the opposite direction lost control of her car, crossed the grassy median and slammed into Hitzges' car head-on. The woman died, and Hitzges broke nearly every bone in his body from the waist up, including a fractured skull.

"I went to the hospital and had all sorts of fractures: fingers, kneecaps, ribs. . . . One of my ribs snapped and punctured my lung," Hitzges said. "They cut off my clothes in the emergency room, and a priest gave me last rites. I didn't have any idea how hurt I was [at first], but when the priest came in I had a pretty good idea.

"But then the doctor came in and said he thought I was going to be OK," he said. "I needed a little more certainty than that, and he said I had broken or fractured more bones than he'd seen in a while, but I'd make it."

By the time his fractured skull stabilized and the doctors were certain no brain fluids were leaking, the remainder of his fractures had pretty much healed. He was in the hospital for two and a half weeks, but he would have been out sooner had it not been for a series of infections in his right arm. He had tried to brace himself in the crash, and his arm had smashed through the windshield, ripping out a chunk of flesh that would later cause the complications.

Hitzges finally left the hospital, but he was in no shape, health-wise or financially, to go back to school. He was able to sleep on a friend's couch for a couple of weeks, and he had about $200 to his name. "Then I said, 'I gotta do something here,'" Hitzges said. "Gas was only about 30 cents a gallon then, and I had a Jensen Healey that was really gas efficient. One place you can stay when you don't have any money is the beach."

So that's where he went—Malaquite Beach near Port Aransas, to be exact.

"I hung out, wrote poems and ate at a $1.59 all-you-can-eat buffet every day at Mrs. Pete's Café," Hitzges said. "It was great; I ate everything I could, crackers and all. I shot some pool at the Sail Club at night.

"When it was time to sleep, I'd park my car against the wind and put a suitcase under the car so that the wind wouldn't whip under it. Then I'd go to sleep on the beach," he said. "The cops never hassled me; it was great."

Hitzges is well known for his compassion toward those down on their luck, as evidenced by the yearly "Normathon" that takes place

"'Preciate ya, pal." Norm and Mean Joe Green.

around Christmas. On that day Hitzges broadcasts for about eighteen hours straight in an event that benefits Dallas' Austin Street Shelter. You would think his stint on the beach would have been the cause of his kind feelings toward the homeless, but that's only partially true.

"It may have a little to do with it; you certainly realize what can happen when you go through periods of your life where you have no money," Hitzges said. "My mom, bless her soul, she and my dad were both children of the Depression. They lived poverty, just like everybody in America at that time.

"I still laugh about it today," he continued. "My mom, when we'd finish a meal in a restaurant, she'd scoop all the Saltines into her purse. She'd say, 'Hey, that came with the meal. That's ours.' She'd wrap up any leftover bread and put it in her purse as well. Maybe that's where some of the empathy comes from.

"But how far from that are any of us?" he added. "You get dealt a hand in life. I used to look down on people like that; even though I didn't have anything myself, I thought they were just bums. But God deals odd hands in life. The people who run the Austin Street

Shelter do incredible work with people who can't take care of themselves. They're depressed, chemically imbalanced, addicted and their families don't want them. The stories of people who have been just dumped out of cars at the shelter are just gut-wrenching.

"So yeah, my own experiences and those of my parents have something to do with it, but I've also come to respect the people who run that shelter so much. It's obvious it's a labor of love."

Back to Hitzges' own story. He spent six weeks on the beach, then decided it was time to re-join the real world. He was able to make it back to grad school at UT by scraping by on odd jobs. It helped that he was living with two other guys in a $90-a-month apartment.

Welcome to Big D

As part of his graduate work, Hitzges was assigned a paper that required him to drive to Dallas and interview Eddie Barker, who was the news director and lead anchor with KDFW-TV (Channel 4). After the interview was done, Barker must have been impressed with Hitzges because he asked him to do a "tape test," or audition, for a spot on the station. Hitzges wasn't exactly dressed for the test—wearing a western shirt and "wheat jeans"—but he aced the test anyway. Barker asked him if he could start immediately, and Hitzges' broadcasting career began on January 10, 1972.

"I did street reporting and sports reporting," Hitzges said. "I didn't like street reporting; I covered a fire where there was a dead person, and I hated it. I went to city council meetings and would nod off."

Enter the late Dick Risenhoover, Channel 4's sports anchor. Risenhoover, who was also the voice of the Texas Rangers for several years in the seventies, pulled the frustrated Hitzges aside one night after a broadcast and hatched a plan over a few beers at The Green Glass, a nearby bar.

"He said he really appreciated how hard I was trying, and that he knew I only wanted to do sports," Hitzges said. "He asked me if I could do four sports stories a day—plot them out, schedule them, shoot them, come back to the studio and write and record the script.

"I said, 'I'll sure try.'"

Risenhoover's idea was for Hitzges to file so many sports stories that the news department would eventually lose track of him, and simply assume Hitzges was "a sports guy." And sure enough, the plan worked. Within three weeks, Hitzges was the sole property of the sports department.

He lasted at Channel 4 until 1975, when new ownership came in and basically cleaned house. But Hitzges was fine, since he had built a pretty lucrative freelance business. Not only was he doing stories for Channel 4, he was also doing stories for CBS, UPI Television and a host of other news organizations. During Hitzges' last year at Channel 4, he estimates that he sold about a hundred stories. The loss of the Channel 4 paycheck hurt, of course, but he wasn't exactly forced to sleep on the beach again as a result.

Radio days

In August of 1975, Tony Garrett became program director at KERA-FM. Garrett remembered Hitzges from their days at Channel 4 and asked him if he'd be interested in doing an hour of sports on Friday mornings—for the staggering total of fifteen bucks a week.

"It was great," Hitzges said. "I must have walked in there [the first day] with five thousand notes. How can you do an hour by yourself without a load of notes? Anyway, after the show Tony walked up to me and asked if I wanted to do the show the next week. I of course said I did, and he said, 'Fine. Then throw away all those damn notes.' He said he'd allow me one page, and to this day that's how I work."

Hitzges writes his notes on a yellow legal pad housed in a worn leather organizer he's had since 1981. "Worn" is putting it mildly—it's surprising that the thing hasn't totally disintegrated. Flip it open, however, and you'll see some Bible verses taped to the inside, as well as a 1974 news clipping from the *Dunkirk Evening Observer* telling of the day Hitzges' father Edgar and a friend saved the life of a man who had tripped and caught some railroad ties. (They had pulled him off the track seconds before an eastbound train roared by.) Hitzges came dangerously close to losing his organizer after leaving on a flight from New York in April of 2008, but someone cleaning the plane was kind enough to turn it in, and it was ultimately returned to him.

He didn't have the pad at the time he started at KERA, but he was making history. Ever since his first day at KERA—August 10, 1975—Hitzges has been on the air in Dallas in one form or another. He kept calling in to the station on Fridays, even when he moved to New York two years later to work for Newsweek TV. Back in those days local TV stations would pay Newsweek $400 a week for feature content. The stations would get fourteen stories a week, ranging from news to business to entertainment to sports. Hitzges did all the sports stories plus a few of the others, giving him a sort of national broadcast presence. After all, about 180 stations around the country used the Newsweek service.

Hitzges did that for two years, then went to Los Angeles to work as executive sports producer for KABC-TV. Still, he'd do the KERA show every Friday.

Welcome home

Hitzges finally returned to Dallas in June of 1980 to take a job talking sports at WFAA-AM. The station was trying to compete with talk powerhouse KRLD-AM, but wasn't doing very well at it. Hitzges was able to make it three years, however, and his ratings were good. But WFAA execs found out the hard way that doing all news and talk can get very expensive, very fast.

Seeing where the station was headed, Hitzges jumped at the opportunity to go to WBAP-AM when he was asked to host an evening sports talk show in 1983. *Sports at Six* would soon become a Dallas radio institution; Ticket hosts Craig Miller and George Dunham listened religiously as kids, and Miller even prank-called Hitzges on a regular basis, as discussed in the previous section.

Although Hitzges was a success on the air, he was miserable about his job. Let's just say he was a little disillusioned with how he was treated by WBAP brass.

"I was naïve enough to believe promises that were made to me by the general manager and the program director," Hitzges said. "I was getting more and more opportunities to do play-by-play: football, soccer, all kinds of stuff. I asked the bosses before I took the WBAP job if it would be OK to accept those play-by-play jobs, and they said they would be all for it as long as there wasn't a conflict.

"My first month there I submitted nine assignments I wanted to do, and they said no to eight of them," he said. "They said, 'We don't want to share our talent.' Was I stupid for not having a contract that would allow me to do the play-by-play I wanted to? Yeah. I had to get out of there as soon as possible."

He didn't have to wait long. Home Sports Entertainment, a cable sports channel focusing on Texas and southwest sports, called Hitzges six months later and asked if he could do some games. He asked them if they needed a sports director. They were stunned that Hitzges would leave WBAP, but he leaped at the chance.

"That started just a spectacular run," Hitzges said. "I loved that job; [fellow HSE broadcasters] Bill Worrell, Greg Lucas and myself got to do everything. Greg even did the Hotter 'N' Hell bicycle race and the Aggie Bonfire. How do you call play-by-play at a bonfire?

"We did little stuff, big stuff...we were flying around to do boxing events from hotel ballrooms—weird, wonderful stuff," he said. "I got to interview Willie Nelson at halftime [during] a college football game. I did Rangers games. It was great."

Despite all the fun he was having, Hitzges still missed being on the radio as much as he had been. In 1985 Dan Bennett, the general manager of KLIF, asked if he was interested in joining the station, which had recently changed to an all-talk format. He asked HSE if they would be OK with it, and they gave him permission—as long as he wasn't working afternoons.

Norm hangs with Swannie.

And thus a conundrum was created. If he couldn't work after-noons, he couldn't get back in radio. Well, how about a morning sports show?

"Dan kicked around the idea a little bit and we ended up starting one in January of 1986," Hitzges said. "I was on a massive travel schedule for HSE, doing about a hundred events. But KLIF would let me travel with equipment and do shows from out of town. It was hellacious, but it was fun."

Hitzges left HSE (which would later become Fox Sports South-west) in 1990 for ESPN. It was the network's first year of airing baseball, and Hitzges was hired as an analyst—the first non-jock analyst on network television since Howard Cosell. He worked pri-marily with Gary Thorne but would occasionally be in a three-man booth, sometimes with Thorne and Joe Morgan and at other times with Thorne and Jim Palmer. He worked games on Wednesday and Friday nights.

And still, all the while, he kept doing his KLIF morning show.

"It was just incredible traveling around the country," Hitzges said. "I'd do a game at Fenway at night, then go back the next morning, set up the equipment to do the KVIL show, then pre-arrange a cab to take me to the airport to go home. I'd spend Thursday and Friday mornings in Dallas and then get right to the airport [because] I was doing an ESPN game that night."

And it wore him the hell out. He stayed with ESPN for seven years, taking on all sorts of assignments. He was doing College Gameday well before the network had ever heard of Kirk Herbstreit or Chris Fowler. He worked horse-racing telecasts. He handicapped football games on Saturday and Sunday mornings.

"By then I was wasted," Hitzges said. "I was actually doing three jobs for a while: mornings at KVIL, ESPN and also doing Rangers games for HSE."

He finally parted ways with ESPN in 1996. But during all that time, he'd been watching developments at The Ticket from afar.

Crossing swords

By then Hitzges and Gordon Keith were firing salvos at each other across the dial on a regular basis. "The day John F. Kennedy Jr. died, he made some remarks I considered to be in very poor taste," Hitzges said. "I laid into him the following Monday.

"Of course, he fired back. Then there was the Fake Norm and Andy Panda. To tell the truth, though, some of that stuff made me laugh. I didn't want to be *seen* laughing, but I was thinking, 'Boy, they've nailed me.' They had a whole bunch of my idiosyncrasies down."

Little did he know he'd be joining Keith and the rest of his nemeses very soon. KLIF dumped sports talk in 2000, and Hitzges had two choices: either leave the company and sit out for six months to honor a non-compete contract, or bite the bullet and head to the thirteenth floor.

"Dan Bennett told me I could work anywhere in Dallas after six months, but there wasn't really anything else here," Hitzges said. "And I didn't want to go out of town.

"There were still things about The Ticket I didn't like, but I worked for a wonderful company and a wonderful boss," he said. "I didn't debate over it. Some members of the staff left me messages, especially Rhynes and Greggo. They told me I'd like it there, that I was coming into friendly territory. They said, 'Come on and join us.'

"There were still obvious issues," Hitzges added. "Gordon and I crossed swords a little bit in the crosstalk. But I have become an unabashed admirer of the guys at The Ticket. It doesn't sound like they put in a lot of work, but they do. I thought those guys were just showing up and taking money."

Hitzges is still amazed at the amount of time that hosts spend doing promotions such as roadshows, Ticketstocks, Ticket Compounds, Summer Bash, Guys' Night Out, Girls' Night Out, and station hockey, football and baseball games. He thinks the station, at times, can take up too much of the hosts' lives.

"I've literally written notes to Cat saying, 'Enough of this. This is crossing the line, abusing our time,'" Hitzges said. "There are about forty days a year that either the entire night or the entire day is devoted to something for The Ticket.

"Not to be money hungry or anything, but we don't get paid for any of it," he said. "We do that stuff because that's the way you develop a radio station. That's where you reach out and touch people. They think they're becoming a better and better friend of yours, which they are. I know hundreds of P1s by name and face."

The health scare of a lifetime

For quite a while in 2003, Hitzges couldn't get out and about to meet anyone. Could barely get out of bed, in fact. After deciding he could no longer stand the excruciating back and leg pain he was suffering, Hitzges finally went to get checked out. What he heard scared the hell out of him.

Hitzges was diagnosed with a tumor at the base of his spine. His surgeon for the incredibly risky procedure, Mike Desaloms, could not guarantee Hitzges would even live, much less walk again. The doctor who diagnosed the tumor, Drew Dossett, gave Hitzges an 80/20 chance of surviving.

"I didn't hear the 80," Hitzges said. "I told [fellow horseplayer and friend] Ponti Campagna that you hear odds like that and immediately you think of all the four-to-one shots that lost in your life."

Dr. Desaloms told Hitzges he would have to trust him to make some important decisions with his life. The doctor could not biopsy the tumor (which turned out to be benign) until Hitzges was on the operating table, didn't know whether or not he could get all of the tumor (he did) and didn't know what kind of damage the tumor and surgery would cause.

After twenty-five days in the hospital, Hitzges was finally able to return home, from where he broadcast his show for several months. Today he has to walk with a cane and has no feeling in his right leg from the knee down. Despite the nuisance, Hitzges says he feels great—he even plays golf better than ever, due to the fact that he doesn't have as many moving parts to screw up his swing.

Around for the twentieth?

Hitzges has no plans to retire to the golf course permanently anytime soon, and can easily see being around for The Ticket's twentieth anniversary.

"That would make me about seventy," Hitzges said. "I'm in very good health; there's nothing wrong with me at all. And I don't ever want to stop working. If I quit, what would I do? I'd get up early, grab the newspaper and tear it to pieces reading it, then call somebody and talk to them about it. If I'm well I could conceive of still being here, sure."

Someone who had a hard time conceiving of having a radio show in a major market such as Dallas is Bob Sturm, whose career is the definition of tenacity and perseverance.

SECTION FOUR

BaD Radio

11

BOB STURM
The Sports Bully

"I am *not* the guy in the next cubicle."

TO SAY THAT RELIGION is a player in Bob Sturm's life is a tremendous understatement. To say Sturm was, um, somewhat sheltered as a child is also giving short shrift to the degree to which he was basically cut off by his parents from influences of the outside world.

But at the same time, it's not like his father locked young Bob in his bedroom and forced him to memorize Bible passages every night after he finished his homework. Yes, Sturm's upbringing is a curiosity to most, but his parents must have done something right. Sturm has an almost shockingly honed sense of humor, considering how sheltered he was as a child. He's more than comfortable in any social setting, unlike a lot of people raised in a strict religious environment, who would just as soon drink a gallon of vinegar than be forced to mingle with a strange crowd.

In short, Sturm is a well-adjusted individual. Even if basically the only TV he was allowed to watch from the age of five to when he left home was sports, *The Dukes of Hazzard* and *CHiPs*.

The way he was reared wasn't exactly considered out of the norm at his school, Calvary Baptist Christian School, in tiny Sun Prairie, Wisconsin (pop. 20,369 in the 2000 census), a suburb of Madison. But ironically, it was that upbringing, combined with his ability to persevere through two crushing career setbacks, that led Sturm to his dream job at The Ticket.

"The little town in *Footloose* is a pretty good comparison to where I was from," Sturm said. "Dancing was thought of as the end of the world. It was a pretty strict side of the street."

Sturm attended the same small school in Sun Prairie from first grade through high school. From first through sixth grades, amazingly, he never shared a class with more than one other person, a girl named Sandy Purbyfill. And she left at the end of sixth grade.

But luckily for Sturm, who was slated to go through seventh grade flying solo, four new kids moved into the school, including Sally, the girl who would eventually become his wife. He would ultimately graduate high school in a class of seven: six dudes and his future wife. There were only twenty-eight students in the entire high school.

So with that kind of backdrop, it's really not much of a stretch to believe Sturm would have a household ruled by a firm mom and dad.

The evil tube

"My parents wanted to do what they thought was right, so they would follow the advice of pastors along the way. There was a time in the seventies and early eighties where TV was made out to be this evil thing in America," Sturm said. "Maybe it is, I don't know; but I like it.

"Anyway, one day they came home from church and decided that TV may be the downfall of their kids," he added. "So the TV became a fairly rare amusement at our house. I was just a kid; I really didn't care about sports that much. But once that rule was put out, I realized that if I wanted to watch TV, I had to be watching sports. Well, now I wanted to watch sports."

And thus little sports computer Sturm was born.

"I became a sports addict at a very young age, because in a way, sports were my cartoons," he said. "I think [my parents] created a monster, probably. That probably explains why I'm obsessed with sports even at age thirty-six. Here I am still going from one sport to the next, and I enjoy all of them. This catalog of useless information in my head is all thanks to my parents, and even my pastor."

Unfortunately, it also made Sturm a pop culture idiot, one who had barely ever heard of the Beatles until *The Hardline* forced him to listen to a song. He could tell you who the top ten NFL rushers were in the 1978 season, but he hasn't a clue about any of the Top 10 movies or albums for that year.

No *Electric Company*. No *Sesame Street*. Not even *Zoom*. None of that mind-warping kids television for the young Sturminator. The embargo lasted all the way through high school for Sturm, although his parents did lighten up a little and let him watch *The Cosby Show*.

Greggo looks away as Bob and Razor compare their flexibility at Charity Challenge on Ice.

So for Sturm, his entertainment was absorbing as much sports minutiae as he could. Whether it was from TV, newspapers, radio, the backs of baseball cards, the books his parents bought for him or the occasional media guide he'd win by calling in to a Madison sports talk show, the information he acquired fueled what would become a lifelong obsession.

But obsession isn't exactly unique in the Sturm family. His father, for example, is consumed by trains. "I think we have this quality in our family, at least among the males, where we find something that encompasses our lives," Sturm said. "On our list of hobbies we may only have one thing, but we go nuts for it. You should see my dad's train collection, and the thousands and thousands of pictures of trains he has.

"When he goes on vacation, he goes to see trains. He would take me on these trips during the summer in Wisconsin and Iowa to take pictures of trains for four or five days," he said. "I'd go because I was seven and had nothing else to do.

"It was cool; we'd go to hotels and eat in restaurants," Sturm added. "But in between meals we were out in the country waiting for a train to go by. He was taking pictures and I was swatting flies. Well, one of these pictures showed me reading a *Sport* magazine. He was trying to introduce me to his trains, and I was sitting there reading the 1979 NFL preview. It's just who I was."

Taking into account Sturm's childhood and the extremely limited exposure he had to the world growing up, it's hard to imagine how he became a polished sports radio talk-show co-host with a subtle yet biting sense of humor. It would seem that people raised like that would run to the nearest corner and roll themselves up into a ball when meeting anyone out of their microscopic circle.

"There are a lot of people with my background who are—for lack of a better term—socially retarded," Sturm said. "I don't have any explanation for why I turned out the way I did. I'm not Mr. Social Butterfly or anything like that, but I do think I can function in life and have the ability to communicate in an effective way.

"It's hard to examine yourself; it's almost impossible to explain things like this," he said. "I only dated one girl, and I was sixteen before I kissed her. It's a weird story, but it's the only one I know so it's not weird to me."

As odd as it may seem to those observing from the outside, Sturm has no regrets about how he was brought up. Especially considering how ecstatic he is today. "I can't imagine a happier existence. I feel sorry for people who find their way to an unbelievable job and are still miserable," Sturm said. "I laugh all day at work; I have a job where when I go on vacation it's not as good as when I'm at work.

"I couldn't second-guess a thing if it got me here."

That's easy for Sturm to say now, but what if he was selling insurance in Madison instead? He came within a hair's breadth of such a fate after two devastating rejections nearly drove him out of broadcasting completely.

Sturm went to Liberty, a Christian university in Lynchburg, Virginia, which was founded in 1971 by Jerry Falwell. Sturm, an excellent basketball player in high school, was unable to crack the Liberty team, so he turned his focus to making a living out of his sports obsession. Four days before graduating from Liberty he accepted a job with Lynchburg's WLNI-FM, otherwise known as "105.9 The Line."

Sturm was a big deal in Lynchburg, no question. He was Mr. Sports Radio. He played golf for free because the course pro liked his show. He rarely paid for a meal in town because so many restaurant owners liked his show.

That gratis treatment was not only much appreciated, it was much needed. To put it mildly, Sturm and his wife were struggling financially. Sturm had to put his IRS payment and car repair bills on his Visa, and the limit on that card wasn't very high to start with. The station was paying him a salary right at the poverty line, and even regular paychecks were no certain thing after a while, as the station began to falter. It was time to make a move.

"About two years into my time at WLNI, I started becoming obsessed with what was coming next," Sturm said. "I would see the old sportswriter in the city who had been there forty-five years, and that started freaking me out. I didn't want to be that guy who was in a city of fifty or sixty thousand, and forty years later they're honoring him. I didn't want to be in a town where the biggest thing was the high school football team. More power to those who can do that, but I couldn't. I had to get to the pros somehow."

Crushing setback No. 1

Sturm's first avenue out of Lynchburg would have taken him out of radio altogether, but for a sports dork like him it would have been a phenomenal job. He found out through a friend that ESPN was looking for an NFL researcher for its *NFL Countdown* and *NFL Prime Time* shows. His paycheck would come from Stats, Inc., but he'd really be working for the likes of Chris Berman and Tom Jackson. The pay would be double that of WLNI—which still wasn't much, but sounded like a ton of money to Sturm—and he'd get to live in Connecticut. He would never be on the air again, but that didn't matter. Instead of *Stump the Schwab* on ESPN, the show might well have been called *Stump the Sturm*.

But it didn't happen. Sturm obviously knew his NFL, that wasn't the problem. It was a pesky little lack of a certain type of computer knowledge that torpedoed his chances in Bristol.

"They gave me two tests. One was on football knowledge—who's the defensive coordinator for the San Diego Chargers, who's the all-time leader in field goal percentage—fairly hard NFL trivia questions," Sturm said. "I got twenty-four out of the twenty-five answers right; they said I had the best score on that test out of anybody.

"But the other test was on computer acumen to design databases, and I knew nothing about that," he said. "I told them, 'I'm your football guy—I swear I am. Give me the job and I'll figure out this database thing.' But they told me they needed somebody to do both, and I went back to Lynchburg.

"I was all excited. I mean, I was going to work at ESPN! This was going to be unbelievable," he said. "Researching football at ESPN? Are you kidding me? I would have done that in a heartbeat."

Sturm was devastated. "I'd been doing my own show for two years, and people were telling me how great I was. In reality I wasn't, but to them I was. Lynchburg had never had a daily sports talk show and it was a neat thing for them. I was a big fish in a small pond, and I still didn't know how to get from Point A to Point B."

Swatted out to mid-court again

In radio, just like almost any other industry, there are various trade magazines that will keep you informed of job openings throughout the country. By now Sturm was desperate to get out of Lynchburg, craving any opportunity—and he didn't care where it was. He ran across an opening in Salt Lake City, where a station needed someone to handle Utah Jazz post-game shows as well as a daily on-air shift.

It was a great time for Sturm, but only from a sports perspective. His favorite team from childhood, the Green Bay Packers, was preparing to play the New England Patriots in Super Bowl XXXI. His hero, Brett Favre, was about to take the field. Just hours before kickoff, Sturm's phone rang. It was Scott Masteller, the program director of the Salt Lake City station. (Masteller would eventually take the program director reins at ESPN Radio in Dallas.)

"He told me he had received my tape and he liked it, and he wanted to fly me to Salt Lake City because he thought I was what they needed," Sturm said. "He said he felt really good about it. Hey, I was in Lynchburg; Salt Lake City sounded great. I hung up and watched the Packers win the Super Bowl. I couldn't have been any more excited.

"And I never heard from Scott Masteller again."

Devastated for a second time and still barely scraping by, Sturm and his wife, who was substitute teaching, came to a decision. "We really missed home; we wanted to get back to Wisconsin," he said. "Now I was contemplating that I just needed to get a job, selling insurance or whatever. Just go back to Wisconsin and live happily ever after, whatever that means.

"It was 1998, and I had been in Lynchburg four years," Sturm said. "I was totally freaking out that my life was trickling away at age twenty-six."

As previously mentioned, WLNI was having a serious problem making payroll, and Sturm was barely above the poverty level as it was. So he camped out in front of his computer in an effort to utilize the Internet to find a way out of Lynchburg. He didn't have anything to lose, as the conventional means of job seeking had proven disastrous.

According to a trade magazine Sturm read, radio personalities seeking to move to more lucrative markets should try to improve twenty to thirty notches at a time. Lynchburg was No. 166 at the time, so a "reasonable" upward move would have been to a market like Dayton, Ohio or, as it happened, Madison. He figured it would be at least ten years before he would hit the Big Time—if ever.

But Sturm came across a Web site, simply titled sportsradio.com, that would soon change his life in ways he could never have imagined. It was run by industry consultant Rick Scott.

"I e-mailed him and said I really felt I had something, but I was sending out tape after tape after tape and I wasn't getting any response at all," Sturm said. "I felt that people were just throwing away tapes without listening to them, much like I did in Lynchburg when I received tapes. They wanted my job; I wasn't going to give them the chance.

"Anyway, he said he wanted me to send him a tape," he said. "I got back in touch with him and he said my tape sounded good. He said a program director from a Top 10 market would be calling me within two weeks.

"A Top 10 market? How is that possible?" Sturm said. "Well, thirteen days later I got a call."

Remember that at this time Sturm and his wife had pretty much accepted their fate, and were resigned to the fact that Bob would never make it in radio. He'd have to give up his dream of making a living in sports. The couple decided to do a little traveling, and see some of the East Coast cities they'd never visited, figuring they'd never get the chance again.

But Sturm was about to get The Call That Changed Everything.

Sturm and his wife were in New York City when Bruce Gilbert called, offering to fly Sturm to Dallas for a tryout. It was Father's Day weekend of '98 and Sturm had his shot. He was scheduled to do a two-hour trial show.

"About an hour and twenty minutes into it [then-assistant program director Jeff] Catlin walks in during a commercial break and says, 'We've got all we need, thanks,'" Sturm said. "It was like *American Idol*, where they stop you in the middle of a song.

"So here I am, in a city I've never been in, doing a show by myself, trying to talk sports," he said. "They cut me off and immediately took me back to the airport. On the way there, I'm searching for a hint from Jeff. Did I do well or did I tank? What was it? I couldn't get anything out of Cat; to this day he doesn't drop his guard. He'd probably be great at poker."

The next morning Sturm sent Gilbert an e-mail consisting of the usual blah, blah, blah. You know, "Thanks for seeing me." He was looking for a response that would provide some sort of clue to what Gilbert was thinking. No such luck. "Hey Bob, thanks for coming out. I'll be in touch" was about all he got back.

The Sturms had decided to go back to Wisconsin if the shot at Dallas didn't work out. No questions asked, no vacillation. No matter what, they were clearing out of Lynchburg. "There was a level of excitement of moving back to friends and family," Sturm said. "Maybe I was never going to broadcast again, but that wasn't a big priority with anybody. I was just twenty-six; I had my whole life before me; big deal.

"The family was like, 'He tried. If Bob has to come back and get a normal job like the rest of us, that's not going to kill him. We're just happy that we're going to get little Sally and little Bob back living with us.'"

It was nearly a month after Sturm's meeting with Gilbert. At another of their East Coast last-chance sightseeing trips, this one on the Mall in Washington, D.C., Sturm and his wife sat on a blanket about to watch fireworks. While they were waiting for the show to begin, Sturm said he figured they were on their way back home.

"This was the 4th of July and I hadn't heard anything since Father's Day," Sturm said. "I was all set to tell the [Lynchburg] station I was going back home and that was that."

Not so fast, Bob

But on the following Monday the seas parted and the skies miraculously cleared, because Gilbert called with an offer to come to Dallas. "They could have offered anything, and I would have said yes. And they did, by the way," Sturm said. "But what did I care? I was [going to be] working in Dallas."

Sturm finally put in his notice to the Lynchburg station and got the hell out. After fifty months and countless hours of worry and bitter disappointment, it was time to turn pro. He and his wife drove halfway across the country, arrived in Addison on a Sunday night, had dinner with Gilbert and his wife, and Sturm reported to his dream gig the next day.

Of course, even though he had spent more than four years toiling in the low minor leagues of radio, Sturm still had to pay his dues once he arrived at The Ticket. He was immediately placed in the black hole of The Ticket programming day, the 8–11 P.M. weeknight slot. It was a strange time work-wise for Sturm; he was on the air every night for two months and then had nearly an entire month off, because The Ticket aired major-league baseball playoff games during his shift in October.

But then mid-day host Rocco Pendola was dumped, and Sturm was given the opportunity to perform in front of an actual audience. Even then, though, Sturm was in flux in terms of his on-air partner. Several people rolled in and out of the co-host chair, including former Dallas television sports anchor Timm Matthews, longtime Ticket personality Mark Elfenbein, former Ticket ticker guy and current Dallas Mavericks play-by-play announcer Mark Followill and a lady named C.J. Silas, who lasted about long enough to have a cup of coffee at the station.

"She was a nice enough girl, but you could tell from the vibe between us that it just didn't make any sense," Sturm said. "You wonder about a woman host at The Ticket and how that would work."

Through all the uncertainty, however, Sturm was ecstatic. He could have shared a studio with a monkey and seven midgets and still been incredibly happy.

"It was unbelievable. Here I was, someone obsessed all my life with getting to a major sports city, and I had finally made it to the big time," he said. "I was on cloud nine; it was the greatest thing ever."

Hello, Dan

Finally, after the parade of co-hosts came through the mid-day shift, Gilbert introduced Sturm to the man who would become his on-air partner for more than ten years, Dan McDowell. At first, Sturm was rather underwhelmed.

"My first impression was, 'I don't get this—at all,'" Sturm said. "If they had given me the choice, I would have done my show with Followill. He and I were just alike; we both wanted to talk straight sports all the time. It was going to be *sports*. We were going to talk Emmitt vs. Barry, argue the DH, talk about whether Pete Rose should be in the Hall of Fame. It was going to be so *sportsy*. It was going to be *great*.

"But Bruce is a brilliant man and I owe him a ton. If it hadn't been for him, I would have been out of radio," Sturm added. "He knew that an ensemble show appeals to more people, because some people are going to love you and others will hate you. But if you have another guy who's different from you, some people will love him and hate him as well. If there's just one of you, or the other guy is just like you, and a listener doesn't like either one of you, he's not going to listen unless he just likes to be driven crazy.

"Whether you love me and hate Dan, or vice versa, [our show] will appeal to more people than a show with me and Mark would have. Bruce knew if I had done a show with Mark that show would have lasted about two weeks."

That's easy for Sturm to say now, but at the time he wasn't exactly thrilled at being partnered with McDowell, who was definitely not a sports almanac. The pairing made no sense to Sturm at all, at the time.

"But Dan had—and still has—a quality where he's largely unaffected by anything around him," Sturm said. "When you can tell I'm excited to be in Dallas doing what I do, you wonder if Dan's excited enough to even be breathing.

"Dan's a different animal, but what's great about him is he's going to tell you what he thinks," he said. "He's not going to put on a big façade. Dan would not be a good politician, but he's great at what he does. I can't put into words how much of a long shot I thought it would be that me and Dan would mesh, but I also can't tell you how great it is to work with the guy.

"Even our bosses don't know what Dan does," Sturm added. "To this day, without naming names, there are people in high places who still question his value. But he's a great deceiver; I don't know anybody who works harder, and I don't know anyone more obsessed with the show. You have to, I suppose, be there to know it. Like I say, even the bosses who are there don't know it. They just sit in their office and listen over the speaker.

"They think I have to hit Dan with a cattle prod to get him to do what he does. It's ridiculous. I would have never selected him in a million years to work with, but I can't describe how much he's done to help get our show to where it is. He's really, really good at what he does."

Know your role

Even after more than ten years as a ratings winner in his time slot, Sturm knows there's still a pecking order at The Ticket. It may be subtle, it may be unspoken, but he knows Mike Rhyner, Craig Miller and George Dunham will always be the station's "A" players. And Sturm is just fine with that.

"It's a weird thing working where we work because everyone up there is so successful," Sturm said. "They have so many skins on the wall that even when you start to put skins on the wall yourself, you're quickly reminded you're still the lowest guy on the totem pole. Here [Dan and I] are, ten years into it, and on some levels we're one of the guys, but on other levels we're still the rookies.

"I don't blame anyone for having the opinion. I feel like I got traded to the Yankees. There's a batting order, no doubt; we happily accept it and totally understand," he said. "But how many others have been in this shift and tried to live up to the standards of The Musers and *The Hardline* and could never hang with those guys? I'm not saying we ever did, but I don't think we would have been here ten years later if we weren't doing well."

The future

Nobody knows where they'll be ten, twenty or more years from now, but if Sturm has his choice, he'll still be exactly where he is now: in The Ticket studio.

"Do I see myself doing anything else? I sure hope not," Sturm said. "Relatives ask me what's next, and I tell them I don't know. It's been so long since I thought about working anywhere else, because this is the destination, I think.

"Will I retire at The Ticket? I hope so, but who knows?" he said. "If it were up to me, I'd capture this moment and never change. People say your years in high school are your greatest years, but forget that. These are the greatest years for me, right here."

And if, however many years later, he's still paired with the subject of the next chapter, Dan McDowell, all the better.

12

DAN McDOWELL

Sports Humorist

"I thought we were having fun here."

I F IT WEREN'T FOR A CALL that came out of the blue one day, Dan McDowell might still be scraping by at an Ohio radio station, pulling down a couple of grand a month and worrying if his car was going to be repossessed. Or he might be cracking jokes on stage in some Cleveland dive, hoping that somebody important would like his shtick and give him his big break.

You didn't know McDowell took a swim through a small-time comedy circuit at one time? Stay tuned. There'll be much more on that later.

At first McDowell wanted to be a pro baseball player, like most kids his age. But, like the vast majority of those kids, he realized by the time he finished Little League that he had no skills. So he adjusted his sights and set them on a career as a pro baseball announcer. That decision set him down a road that wound through some Podunk Ohio towns and chump-change radio gigs, but it ultimately led him to Dallas.

Welcome to McConnelsville

McDowell's first job out of Ohio University was in the village—yes, *village*—of McConnelsville, Ohio, located in the southeastern corner of the state. To get a feel for how small this place is, according to 2000 census figures, the population was 1,676. And McDowell was there nearly ten years prior to that, in 1992.

The station, WJAW-AM, was named after owner John A. Wharff, the longtime voice of the Ohio State Buckeyes. The McConnelsville station was actually a satellite of a larger station in the Ohio metropolis of Marietta. McDowell was part sales guy, part play-by-play guy. His base of operations was the bedroom of an apartment located in McConnelsville's downtown square, directly above a sewing store.

The station offered him a thousand a month coming right out of college, plus commission on sales and a free apartment. He could do as much play-by-play as he wanted of area high school sports, and he would also be the news guy. McDowell would do the 6 and 7 A.M. newscasts, reading out of the paper. They'd then simulcast easy listening music out of Marietta the rest of the day.

"All that so McConnelsville residents could be proud of the fact that they had their own station," McDowell said. "I'd wake up, go into the other bedroom, fire up the dials and be on the air. We had a thermometer outside the window. That was the WJAW Weather Center.

"But it was good times, and it gave me a lot of experience," he added.

McDowell left WJAW to work for WATH, an AM station in Athens near Ohio University. Once again he did high school football and baseball and sold advertising. He even had the title of Sports Director. He would soon find out the hard way, however, how small minds often rule small towns.

"It was going swimmingly. I did about a year of play-by-play and sales," McDowell said. "This was a very depressed area surrounding Athens, like the front porch scene in *Deliverance*. It was bad.

"Anyway, Athens was taking on Trimble in a football game. The Trimble Tomcats. They would do a morning back-and-forth on the local FM station about what was going on that night," he said. "I said Athens was taking on 'the scummy Trimble Tomcats and we hope to get a victory.'"

You talking about me?

It turns out that the good folks of Trimble are a little sensitive to words like "scummy" being used to describe them. After all, the hottest business in town is selling plywood for use in boarding up foreclosed homes. It wasn't long before someone got wind of the slight and complained to the station.

"Later in the day I'm doing my thing—I'd drive to a sales call, write it down in my log and then not go in. I hated sales," McDowell said. "The program director called me in, saying there was a big thing at the school. They were ready to protest at the game. Remember, this is a very depressed area, and some local broadcaster is calling them 'scummy.'

"The program director said not only were they suspending me from the game, I had to go into the locker room to apologize to the team," he said. "It turned into this big thing because of one parent.

"The station didn't stand up for me at all. I went to the locker room, and the kids couldn't have cared less. That's when I knew I had to get out of there."

By this time, McDowell had soured on his second dream, that of being a pro baseball play-by-play guy. He had done hundreds of games by this point, and was, to put it simply, bored. "You couldn't deliver any kind of opinion, couldn't ever say what happened," he said. "If a kid dropped a ball, you had to say something like, 'the wind got a hold of it.' You always had to make excuses. You couldn't say anything that even had a hint of negativism. And I was getting tired of the same old coach interviews.

"A monkey could do play-by-play," McDowell continued. "There are a few good ones who go above and beyond. I think [Texas Rangers play-by-play man] Josh Lewin is great because he does a ton of research. But in general, it's a very lazy profession. 'So, coach, what's the game plan? Good luck.' That kind of stuff. I was getting tired of it. My dream wasn't turning out like I thought it would."

What's the deal with...?

Disgusted with the lack of support provided by WATH management and disillusioned with radio in general, McDowell seriously considered turning in a completely different direction and taking a shot at comedy. He had taken a stand-up comedy class at Ohio U, one of the only programs of its kind offered in the country. The final exam had consisted of doing stand-up at a local bar. McDowell won the contest and the professor asked him if he wanted to join a comedy

Bob and Dan rack it up at Bowling for Spares.

troupe that performed in bars throughout southern Ohio and West Virginia.

"Every weekend there would be two shows. There was a woman, a black guy, a redneck and me, the clean-cut college guy," McDowell said. "I thought about doing it full time, since I was good enough to win the contest. But when you're in radio you can't see somebody turning the dial or turning it off. In comedy, it's hard when you see the crowd not react.

"You learn some tricks, like using profanity," he said. "In those days I thought I could be funny enough without being profane, but drunk rednecks in West Virginia like F-bombs."

McDowell's type of humor was self-deprecating, along the lines of influences such as Gary Shandling and Jerry Seinfeld. "My most memorable line was, 'I'm a little nervous. I'm not really used to holding something this big in my hand [referring to his micro-phone].' It all went downhill from there.

"It's tough to do the same thing over and over, to hone jokes," he said. "Even that little line, saying it only the fifteen or twenty times I did, making it sound [each time] like you're doing it for the first time ever is tough. It's a true skill to make that kind of thing seem spontaneous.

"Anyway, I don't like to talk about it a lot because I was really bad at it. I feel stupid just talking about it. It wasn't for me."

Back to the grind

So much for that slew of *The Tonight Show* appearances that would have led to a massive movie deal. It was back to reality for McDowell, meaning he had to get away from WATH and its milquetoast management. He had started to realize he had something, that he could be compelling on the air. But he still had to wear a tie because he was selling also, and that was making him even more bitter. He was especially bitter toward a "wacky FM guy" who was working across town.

"That guy had a bag," McDowell said. "He was making at least what I was making, and he had a bag of nothing. I had to sell every day, wear a tie and put up with this management crap. My goal was to make money in radio without selling. Even if I never made more than that FM guy, at least I wouldn't have to wear a tie."

So McDowell was able to get a job at an FM station in Zanesville, Ohio. He still made practically nothing, and he still lived in a tiny apartment. But he was co-hosting a morning show. And most importantly, he didn't have to wear a tie anymore.

"My shtick wasn't good. Seriously," McDowell said. "I worked with a girl named Michele who had a glass eye. She really did. I stayed there about six months."

McDowell was briefly able to get back to the big city when a job opened up at Cleveland's WHK. It was going to be a sports-talk format, just about the same time The Ticket started, in 1994. "My friend told me about the job; that they were hiring producers, board ops and ticker guys. He said I'd make crap money, but I was making crap money anyway in Zanesville." The station would only pay for fifteen hours per week, but he worked forty as a sort

of jack-of-all-trades, running the board, producing shows. But he had to downgrade his living arrangement. Instead of living in a station-furnished apartment, he had to hole up in his mother's basement.

But he was in a major market, and eventually he got full-time hours. He even did a weekend show for a while. But the station, he learned, was going to be sold, and its format would become religious broadcasting. Luckily, two WHK sales guys were opening their own station in Warren, Ohio, and they wanted him to come along as the program director.

"They paid nothing, too, but they let me do whatever I wanted. I decided the format, I did the hiring," McDowell said. "I gave myself a talk show. When you have to sit there and fill three hours in Warren, Ohio every day, you learn a lot of things that work and don't work. You learn what kind of guests work, and if you even want guests. What makes the phones go, and whether or not it's important to get the phones going.

"There was a lot of trial and error, but it was fun," he continued. "Again, I wasn't making but one thousand a month, but I had a free apartment and the sales guys got me a good deal on a car."

The dash for Dayton

The turning point in McDowell's career came in 1997. The moment that would indirectly lead him to Dallas was an unexpected call from a program director at a station in Dayton, which is to Warren what Dallas is to Ennis.

"I got a call out of the blue from a guy who just happened to have the same name as a guy we had had on that morning who we thought we had offended," McDowell said. "He said he was in Dayton and he had heard the show. He asked me if I wanted to come to Dayton for a tryout, and I said hell yeah.

"Turned out they had a news guy who had been driving around and heard me," he added. "They had a bad situation there. Just like Rocco [Pendola, McDowell and Bob Sturm's predecessor as midday host at The Ticket], they had a guy everybody hated and they were in a bind. Of all the résumé tapes I sent out, it turns out a call out of the blue got me out of Warren."

But McDowell's good fortune soon turned sour in Dayton, where a micromanaging, meddling program director turned what should have been a good gig into a nightmare.

"It was initially awesome, but I was the only live show, on from three in the afternoon to seven in the evening. The PD didn't have anything to work with besides me," McDowell said. "It was a horrid, really bad year and a half. It was a bunch of me sitting in a room with the program director, listening to tapes, with him picking them apart and telling me what I could have done better. It was the most money I had ever made, but it was terrible. I still got my car repossessed, so the money wasn't that great.

"I got to be creative a little bit," he added, "but they were up my ass a lot."

But that was a mere annoyance for McDowell compared to what would ultimately drive him out of Dayton. Once again, it was a lack of support from management over a seemingly innocuous statement. During a show, McDowell was talking about the singer Neil

Diamond and referred to him as the "Jewish Elvis." That was the beginning of the end.

"Some old person got on his typewriter and wrote a letter of complaint," McDowell said. "When the PD got that, he had me issue an apology on the air. [Station management] was always kind of against me, but they liked me better than the [previous] guy.

"I knew what the deal was. On April Fool's Day in 1999 they called me in and told me they were changing my shift, from 3–7 to 5–9," he said. "I thought it was a prank, that they were recording it. But it wasn't—I wasn't in drive time anymore. They said it wasn't a demotion, but that wasn't the message I was getting. Give me a break."

The big move to Big D

So it was time to update the résumé—again. One of McDowell's childhood friends who had moved to Dallas told him about a new sports radio station called The Ticket. The friend suggested he apply. Then another old friend, someone McDowell had hired at the station in Warren, told him he had applied for a mid-day slot at The Ticket but gotten shot down.

"The guy who had been shot down in Dallas was really impressed with his rejection," McDowell said. "[Former Ticket PD] Bruce Gilbert would listen to tapes, tell you why he didn't like them and tell you what you needed to work on. That just doesn't happen.

"Anyway, I sent him a tape and he responded," he continued. "I sent him a bit where the GM of our station bet me I couldn't run a mile in under ten minutes. I think he really liked it because it wasn't just me doing 'real' radio."

Gilbert asked McDowell to meet him in Indianapolis, and McDowell jumped at the chance. After impressing Gilbert in the first meeting, McDowell had a second interview at The Ticket studios, where he was quickly immersed in what sets the station apart from all the others.

"It was the weekend of the Byron Nelson tournament, the one

where *The Hardline* got in trouble," McDowell said. "They were broadcasting from the tournament, and they were going into their third segment on guessing the bra sizes of the women who were passing by their broadcast booth. Then they'd guess whether the girls' breasts were real or fake.

"I'm thinking, 'This is awesome!'" he said.

McDowell didn't know what kind of show he could get on—or whether he'd have a partner—and he didn't care. He knew he wanted to be at The Ticket. He met Bob Sturm the next day and the two attended a hockey game. Shortly after, Gilbert hired McDowell and *BaD Radio* was born.

"[Sturm] seemed like a good guy, with the same origins I had," recalled McDowell. "It was like we were [both] originally young sports nerds, but he kind of stayed nerdier while I discovered alcohol, drugs and girls.

"Not that we're not still nerds," he added.

Even though McDowell was thankful to be out of Dayton, he still wasn't 100 percent sure he wanted to be partnered with someone. But he knew he was determined to make the pairing a success.

"I was originally under the impression that it would be a one-man thing from noon to three," McDowell said. "He asked how I would feel about working with a partner. You could have asked me anything and I would have agreed to it. I was in *Dayton*.

"I think Bruce thought that Bob's personality and sports background would end up working with mine," he said. "I think if we had more say or any clout we would have objected more, but we were both just happy to be in Dallas. He was happy not to be working nights and I was happy not to be in Dayton. We both really wanted to make it work."

Really *BaD Radio*

Sure, McDowell had doubts as to whether or not the show would succeed. But he soon realized that his and Sturm's visions for the show were similar, even if their personalities were different. They wanted to fit in with the rest of The Ticket shows, but not copy them.

"When we first got there, [Sturm] got the Ticktionary and familiarized himself with Ticket terms, wanting to use them on the air," McDowell said. "I didn't pay attention to that stuff because I figured we'd develop our own thing over time. We had our own things to offer, and we're radio professionals, so we didn't need to be doing what everybody else did."

What made that a little difficult for a while was the presence of Kevin "Expo" Fox as the *BaD Radio* board operator. Expo made a habit of producing drops similar to those he was doing for the other show he worked on, *The Hardline*. McDowell was pretty irritated by this. After all, how was his and Sturm's show going to be able to find its own way if it sounded like the more entrenched drive-time show?

"We didn't like having the same board op as *The Hardline*," McDowell said. "Since he was responsible for a lot of sound for both shows, he copied a lot of what he did for them with us. We didn't want to be a carbon copy. Our rule was no drops of us. We've since blown that out, but for the first few years that was part of what we did to stand out on our own."

But even after the show started to find its legs, McDowell remained distrustful of program directors, due to his bitter experiences in Ohio. He was fully prepared for Gilbert to be the same type of micromanaging, soul-killing presence he had faced in his previous jobs. Even though McDowell had what seemed like his dream job in Dallas, that old apprehension hadn't gone away.

Gilbert erased that after one post-show meeting in the early days of *BaD Radio*.

"Did I think Bruce would micromanage the show? Yes, I did, because in my experience that's what PDs do," McDowell said. "They have nothing; they wish they could do a show but they can't, so they tell you how to do one. If they ever got the opportunity to do one, they'd fall flat on their face. I always considered PDs a nuisance I had to work through.

"But Bruce changed all of that. We sat down after a show and he asked us what we thought," he said. "I went to my Rolodex of what PDs thought, knowing what he'd be looking for. I told him we didn't say the call letters very much and didn't update the time. He goes, 'Look, I don't give a damn about that. That's not your job; that's my job. What about your content, your opinions? Did it go the way you wanted?'

"He said, 'If I could do what you're doing, I'd be doing it," McDowell said. "You think people get into radio wanting to be in management? We all start on the air, and if we can be stars we're going to be. You think players want to be coaches? They want to play.'

"Bruce told me, 'I think certain things work, but sometimes you have to play it by ear,'" McDowell said. 'It's your show. I'll back you up 100 percent. If somebody complains, we won't throw you under the bus.'"

It was then that McDowell realized he had finally found a radio home. He was no longer constricted by small-minded simpletons; he was in the big leagues, and loving every second of it.

Nearly ten years later, he still does. And so does the third guy in the *BaD Radio* booth, Donovan Lewis.

13

DONOVAN LEWIS

Donnie Doo

"It's the GREAT Donovan! WOO!"

I F YOU EVER GET THE CHANCE to corner Donovan Lewis at a roadshow and talk to him about anything, jump at it. There is no more engaging personality at The Ticket—or anywhere else—than Lewis; you'll have a blast talking to him.

But at one point, Lewis was about fifteen minutes from turning his back on the broadcasting business and becoming a teacher. He had completed his certification testing and was ready to make the leap. For sure, Mr. Lewis' class would have been fun, but lucky for Ticket fans, he stuck it out and eventually became an important part of *The Bob and Dan Show*.

Besides Mike Rhyner, Lewis is the only Ticket host born and raised in Dallas. He grew up in Oak Cliff and went to high school at the Business and Management Center, where he vacillated between wanting to become an engineer and satisfying his "finance/banking jones," as he puts it.

"I would have gone to South Oak Cliff for high school, but I was about 5'2" in ninth grade, and I didn't feel like getting my ass whipped every day," Lewis said. "My older sister went to the Center, so I decided to follow her."

"I don't really know why I wanted to be an engineer," he said. "I was always good at math, so I guess one day in elementary school someone said engineers are good in math, so bang—I'm going to be an engineer."

Lewis graduated high school at sixteen, as he was able to skip a grade due to outstanding test scores. "My mom said it would have been awkward for me to graduate at fifteen," Lewis said. "Let me tell you, it wasn't any damn better at sixteen."

Becoming a radio personality wasn't anywhere close to being part of the equation. In fact, the closest Lewis came to being an announcer was when he was seven or eight years old, emulating Verne Lundquist on *Bowling for Dollars*, a popular nightly show on Channel 8 where contestants would get a jackpot for rolling three consecutive strikes. It was a simple premise, but it was must-see TV in the mid to late seventies.

"That was my favorite show growing up," Lewis said. "I had a plastic bowling set. My older sister and I would set it up, and we'd bowl down this long hallway in our house. One of us would bowl, the other would announce. If she was bowling, I'd talk really quietly. 'She's walking up. . . . She's throwing the ball. . . .'

"And everything would be the 7–10 split. *Everything*. She could have five pins sitting there and it would still be the 7–10 split."

Then there was the time he and a friend "played radio" in elementary school. He'd spend the night at his buddy's house, who had a pretty sophisticated audio component set. The friend would plug a microphone into the speakers at about 10:30 on Saturday night. That's when KKDA-FM (K104) would broadcast from a place called Club Starz—"S-T-A-R-Zeeee, *baybayyyy*," as Lewis put it. But Lewis and his buddy would make believe they were broadcasting their own show, from Club Carz.

"C-A-R-Zeeee, *baybayyyy*! We'd do that all night long," Lewis said. "Every time the radio announcers would turn on their mic after a song played, we would, too. His mom would be like, 'Y'all be quiet!' and we'd start whispering. But it wasn't long before we started getting loud again.

"We did that once a month, but when Club Starz went out of business, Club Carz did, too. That was tough to deal with."

Too dA&Mn big

Those were really the only times Lewis even gave a thought to broadcasting. His main plan was still to be an engineer—until one day during his senior year of high school.

"I wanted to go to Texas A&M because I had heard the engineering program there was the best," Lewis said. "I had A&M T-shirts and everything.

"And then one day—Martin Luther King, Jr. Day of my senior year, in fact—we had the day off and our school had a bus trip to College Station," he said. "I've never been that intimidated in my life; everything was so big.

"Our high school had two buildings, an 'A' and a 'B' building," Lewis said. "When we rolled down to A&M, they were talking about 'M' and 'N' buildings. It just scared the hell out of me. So I said, 'OK—that engineering thing at A&M is out the door.'"

Lewis wanted to stay closer to home, so he started considering other options for college. A couple of friends told him about East Texas State University in Commerce, about seventy miles from Dallas (ironically, the school is now known as Texas A&M University–Commerce), and they decided to check it out on a whim one weekend.

"We went there and knocked on a random dorm room," Lewis said. "Some guy answered the door and we told him we were thinking about going to school there. We asked him if we could check out his room. He said sure and invited us in. He even took us around the campus. We loved the place, and it wasn't too far away, so that's where I went."

But he would have to do so as something other than an engineering major.

"I took my first drafting class, which was the hardest class I'd ever taken," Lewis said. "And it was just an introductory class! I talked to a counselor, and I must have just kept going on and on and on, because she said, 'Have you ever thought about broadcasting?'

"I said, 'Not really, but why not?' So I took my first broadcasting class and it was awesome. I was so raw it was unreal, but it was fun."

His first "real" broadcasting gig was being the faceless voice on Commerce Cable Channel 3, a public access channel that basically ran commercials 24/7 for local companies. Music from a local radio station provided the background sound, with news and weather reports interspersed. ETSU freshman broadcasting students provided those reports, and Lewis took his turn. He quickly realized he had a whole lot of work to do.

Nowhere to go but up

"I was bad...*soooo* bad. 'Hello, um, we're, uh, doing the weather. Yeah. It's going to be sunny,'" Lewis said. "I wish I had kept the tapes.

"But I really enjoyed it and caught the broadcasting bug for real," he said. "I just didn't know what exactly I wanted to do. I really wasn't interested in TV; I had developed a fascination for radio. The only TV-related thing I was remotely interested in was working the camera. And I would do that right now—if somebody asked me to do that, I'd be all over it."

While Lewis was having a good time with his classes, he was barely skating by on the bare minimum—doing exactly what he needed to satisfy graduation requirements, but no more. All the other students were getting substantial, hands-on experience, and Lewis was a senior. He knew that had to change, and he found his opportunity when he learned KETR-FM was revamping its high school football broadcast. The station was looking for an entirely new staff—a new play-by-play guy, a new analyst and new sideline reporters.

"I went in for the audition and it was the most nervous I'd ever been in my life," Lewis said. "They said they had something like thirty-five people they were choosing from. Me and this other guy sat down to audition; he was doing play-by-play and I was doing color. But every time it got to be my time to talk, I was so nervous he had to elbow me in the ribs.

"They interviewed us separately afterward and asked me why I should get the job," he said. "I told them I was a senior and I wanted to get more involved in broadcasting. Simple as that. There was no way I was going to get it. None."

The following Thursday the names were posted of the students who earned gigs. Lewis hung back and let the crowd tell him whether he had made the grade. Somebody would say "damn" then somebody else would clap. Then he heard a couple of other claps and a lot more "damn"s. He only heard three claps for five slots, so he figured he had a shot. Sure enough, he had been chosen for a sideline spot.

It was a good thing, too. A couple of days before, Lewis had been told by a professor that he should maybe "find another prospective career," adding that he wasn't really a good fit for broadcasting.

Just the kind of thing you want to hear, right?

"As I was heading to my room after the meeting, I started wondering if he was right," Lewis said. "School had been a little more difficult than I thought it would be, and it was only getting harder. If I hadn't gotten that high school football gig, I would have been too discouraged to go on."

But he did get the gig, and started doing football games for the station. By his own admission, he was raw as hell. That especially showed during an interview with Commerce's head coach after the first game.

"I'm at the middle of the field getting ready to interview him live for the post-game show," Lewis said. "I had my pad with me with all my questions. I walked up to him to introduce myself, said I wanted to interview him, and he said, 'Fine.'

"I asked him the first question. I was so nervous, I just stuck the microphone in his face and kept looking at my pad," he said. "I wasn't even listening to him, because I was looking at the next question. He gave me a one-word answer—'Yes.' I thought he was still talking.

"Then I realized, 'This cat is not talking,'" Lewis added. "I was looking at him, he was looking at me. There was nothing but dead air—remember, this was live. It was awful. He gave me a wink, patted me on the butt and walked off the field. After that he was cool; it was like he was giving me some sort of initiation.

"That was a fun season, and they went pretty far in the playoffs. After that experience, I knew what I wanted to do."

The con is on

Lewis did enough schoolwork to earn the credits he needed to graduate. Well, almost enough.

One of his classes senior year was creative writing. Four papers would determine his grade, and he needed to do well on all of them in order to graduate.

"I did very well on my first three, but this was my last freaking semester, man," Lewis said. "I was partying hard. I procrastinated and procrastinated, and I didn't get that last paper done. And graduation was in a few days.

"But that professor was the most unorganized individual you'll ever find. I went into his office and told him I hadn't gotten my paper back. He said, 'You didn't?' I said, 'No, and I've been waiting for it. I've got to know what my grade is so I know if I can graduate. He started moving papers around on his desk, saying, 'It's got to be here someplace. Look; I'll find it and give it back to you.'

"So now it's graduation day and I'm thinking, 'Did I con this guy? Did it work? Or did he catch on and say, "He never turned in any paper. I'm going to fail his ass."' I had no idea. My parents were there and here I was, not going to graduate. I thought for sure my plan had backfired and my parents were going to kill me."

But not only did the con work, that professor must have felt so bad about "losing" Lewis' paper that he gave him an A.

Welcome to your new life

Lewis often refers to his Uncle Perry on the air. You know, the wise uncle that every family has, the guy who knows all the answers to any question. As a graduation gift, Perry introduced Lewis to Dallas talk-radio icon Bob Ray Sanders, who had a show at KLIF-AM. It may have been the most important lunch of Lewis' life—even to this day. Sanders told Lewis he thought the station was hiring, and it would probably be worth it to apply.

"I got an interview for a board op position," Lewis said. "Everything was great; the lady said I was great and she wanted to hire me. They were going to mail me a work schedule.

"That was on a Thursday. The following Monday I got a letter in the mail on KLIF letterhead," he said. "It read, 'We're sorry to inform you that we have no positions available. We'll keep your résumé on file.' It was a form letter with Dan Bennett's signature on it.

"What the hell was this? They told me I had a job."

It was all a misunderstanding, though, and Lewis showed up the next day. That was one hell of a stressful way to start a radio career, but a start it was. And even though he was only working the board, Lewis realized just how lucky he was to be able to begin his career in a major market.

"When I was in college, the teachers would beat it into our heads that we'd be working overnights in Bugtussle, Texas for minimum wage," Lewis said. "Plus, we'd have to sweep up the station afterward.

"We heard that all the time, and I wasn't prepared to do that," he said. "If that were the case, I'd just do something else. Uncle Perry had his own State Farm office and I figured I'd work there if I had to. But trust me, I knew how lucky I was to get even that board operator job on a Dallas station."

Lewis started as a part-time board op in July of 1993 and became the full-time overnight board op a few months later, working

10 P.M. to 6 A.M., Sunday through Thursday. But he couldn't have cared less that it wasn't exactly a desirable shift. He was working full time and had benefits, and that was all he'd been worried about.

"The Ticket had started about that time, and they were taking some people from KLIF, but I never even interviewed over there. I was happy to be where I was at," Lewis said. "I was eventually able to get off of overnights and work production nine to noon for Kevin McCarthy's show. *Kool and the Gang*. I got off overnights *and* I was making more money. Everything was lovely."

The big break

Lewis worked on the show in silence, with no mention of him ever made and definitely no chance of him actually getting on air. That changed one day, after McCarthy invited Lewis to lunch so he could get to know him a little better.

"We were having fun, joking around, and he said, 'You know, we need to get you on the air more often,'" Lewis said. "I said, 'Let's do it.'

"I started to be part of a daily segment, 'The Show Meeting,' which took up the first thirty minutes, where the hosts talk about what's going on in the world. We really hit it off; it was fun and Kevin was laid back. He'd give me a little advice after the show, and started teaching me the game.

"I had to sit back and realize I was in Dallas, working with a legend and cracking jokes on the air. It was unbelievable."

Lewis worked on McCarthy's show for five years and everything was going fine. But then McCarthy started developing health problems that would plague the show. Some days he couldn't come in at all, then on others he could only do it for thirty minutes before he had to leave. McCarthy was battling a host of ailments, including an inner-ear problem, dizziness and repeated bouts with nausea. The uncertainty surrounding McCarthy wore on Lewis, and all of a sudden he wasn't having such a good time anymore.

Time to bolt

In addition to working with McCarthy, Lewis was also in the "continuity department," basically making sure the right commercials were playing at the right time and making sure the hosts had the correct copy for live commercial spots. And he hated it. Combine that mind-numbing job with the concerns about McCarthy, and Lewis was ready to make a drastic move.

"I was fifteen minutes from leaving," Lewis said. "I had been studying to get a teaching certificate; I had taken all the tests and had all the paperwork done. I had just gotten married, and I needed to start making a little money. I was out.

"It was about time for my lunch break, so I walked down the hall, looked into the program director's office and kind of stopped," he said. "I told him I was about to become a teacher, and he was floored. He asked me, 'If I pay you this much will you stay?' I said, 'For you, yes.'"

Taking one for the team

Lewis had a little more change in his pocket, but the station was crumbling. KLIF let some of their most popular hosts go, including McCarthy, in an effort to improve stagnant ratings. It couldn't have worked out worse, as ratings plummeted to levels no one anticipated. Taxicab frequencies were pulling better numbers than "Big 570," which was the name of the re-tooled station.

"When the format changed, they asked me to produce the morning show," Lewis said. "I was finally out of the continuity department, at least, but Big 570 was a sheer disaster. I wasn't the greatest producer in the world, and I'll admit that, but they wanted me to get in the studio with Joe Kelly. I was thinking, 'What the hell is this? They want me to be a co-host?'

"It was almost like I was set up to fail," he said. "There was no freaking way that was going to work. That political...whatever kind of talk it was, I had no clue about. None. When the Gore/Bush stuff happened in 2000, that was the lead topic for about three or four months. Every day. I was just sitting there; I didn't know what the hell was going on. There was no way I should have been there.

"So I went to the PD and said, 'This isn't me. I'm laying out most of the show. I'm just stealing money, I really am.' They had to know, but nobody ever said a thing."

Everybody who works in radio wants to be on the air. PDs, producers, board ops—everybody. If they tell you different, don't believe them. So what Lewis did next could either be considered career suicide, insanity, absolute idiocy or a combination of all three.

He just thought it was the right thing to do for the station.

"They brought in another guy, Scott Anderson, and they thought I might be a better fit as producer on his morning show," Lewis said. "I said, 'Let's do that.' I was willing to do whatever to get the hell off of that political talk show.

"Scott was fine to work with; he was a good dude," he said. "The board op was a guy named Brian, and he was the best board op I'd ever seen. But he suddenly passed away. When that happened, I went to the PD again and said, 'Look, you can find a better producer. But you won't find a better board op than me. I can run the board; you can find another producer.'"

So, to summarize, first Lewis demoted himself from co-host to producer, and then he demoted himself from producer to board op.

"I didn't think I'd ever get back on the air—anywhere," Lewis said. "But I have the most supportive wife ever, and she didn't have a problem with it."

What the hell did I just do?

Lewis wanted to be a board op, and he got his wish. And he almost immediately started regretting his team-first move. He worked the board for a series of syndicated shows, which meant no interaction with a local host, basically just sitting back and listening. The year was 2002 and Lewis was on the verge of another career crisis.

"I made a decision that if I was still doing this at the end of the year I'd have to leave and do something else," Lewis said. "I was bored as hell, and this job wasn't going anywhere."

Then, seemingly out of the blue, Lewis was given an opportunity that would eventually lead him to The Ticket. Scott Strong, program director at sister station KDBN-FM, otherwise known as The Bone, approached Lewis about a position. Strong wanted him to produce Dallas radio icon Bo Roberts' morning show. But Lewis was hesitant about leaving KLIF, so he didn't immediately commit to the move.

That didn't last long, thanks to some not-so-subtle urging from the top.

"Classic rock? I didn't know anything about it," Lewis said. "He said I didn't need worry, since they'd teach me everything I needed to know about the music. I said I'd think about it.

"Then the boss, Dan Bennett, called and said I really should think seriously about the job, because 'You never know how many more chances you're going to get,'" he said. "My wife said, 'I'm thinking you really need to take that job. They probably don't have anything else for you to do, and you're probably out of options.'

"Great. I'm good. I'll take it."

Resistance on two fronts

One again, Lewis found himself working with a Dallas radio legend he had never heard of. And for the first time, race began to be an issue.

"Of course, it was the oddest fit in the whole wide world, and I got plenty of e-mails wondering, 'What the hell is a black man doing on my classic rock station?'" Lewis said. "There were a lot of calls, and I got the n-word a lot. But I took the high road. I was like, 'If you come up with something new, then I'll be upset. Until then, I'm cool. I've heard it all before.'

"It was addressed a little bit on the air. Bo stood up for me, saying, 'He's here, we're glad to have him,' stuff like that," Lewis said. "If the people you're working with are glad you're there, that's all that matters."

It helped somewhat that Lewis didn't really have a big on-air presence, since he was, of course, the producer of the show. But still, even disregarding the racist e-mails and phone calls from listeners, Lewis still didn't know jack about classic rock.

"I definitely had some learning to do," Lewis said. "One Saturday I went to a Bone event and Scott Strong asked me if I wanted to meet Alice Cooper. I said, 'Sure. Who's she?'"

The real issue facing Lewis, and one more daunting than racist morons or lack of familiarity with the music, was the fact that Roberts really wasn't that crazy about the way Lewis did sports updates. Strong knew Lewis liked sports, and he knew Lewis had something to offer on-air, so he tapped him as the sports guy for the morning show. Previously, the station had brought Rich Phillips over from The Ticket to do those updates. Phillips would do a Ticket Ticker, come over to The Bone, then go back a few minutes later to do another ticker.

Bo didn't like Lewis taking over the sports slot.

"He liked Rich, and he's not well-equipped for change, so it upset him some at first," Lewis said. "I wanted to add a little flavor to the updates, while Rich was more straightforward. Comedy's suggestive, and you're not going to hit a home run every time. But I'm going to keep swinging; I don't give a damn if it's not funny. If it's not, I'll ask for forgiveness.

"Anyway, they fired Bo's co-host and [then] it was just me and him," he said. "I thought it was going fine, but I was getting some signs he didn't like the way it was working out. I talked to him and said if there was something wrong, he needed to tell me. There wasn't any need for him to wait until he couldn't take it anymore and explode, or go to the boss.

"But he kind of warmed up to my approach, then another host was added, Cowboy Bill, and everything was going fine."

Bam!

Then one morning, out of the blue, when the second the show was over the bosses walked into the studio. One boss told Bo to come with him, while the other summoned Donovan to his office.

"Ol' dumb Donovan says, 'OK.' I walked upstairs thinking everything was fine and dandy," Lewis said. "We get to his office and sit there, not saying a word for ten minutes. He'd kind of look over here...then over there...but wouldn't talk. I finally asked him what was going on and he said, 'I'll tell you in a minute.'

"Sixty seconds roll by and I say, 'OK, it's been a minute. What the hell is happening?'" Lewis said. "He finally said, 'We've let Bo go.' It was a total shock; I had no idea. I asked him what it meant for me and he said, 'Nothing. You're good. I just can't tell you anything else right now.'

Ten minutes later the other suits walked in, confirmed the news about Bo and told Lewis that he'd be part of a three-man morning show with Cowboy Bill and former KLIF personality "Humble" Billy Hayes. That would soon turn into a disaster, as tension between Hayes and Cowboy Bill got so intense that the work environment became impossible. Management fired Cowboy Bill, brought in a young guy named Spicoli, then turned around and fired him. It was once again a two-man show with Lewis and Hayes.

Faraway dreams

This was around the time Cumulus Radio bought out Susquehanna Radio, throwing Lewis' career into uncertainty again. It was clear The Bone was faltering, and that everything at the station would soon change.

Even though he hadn't really considered applying to The Ticket, Lewis saw the happiness oozing out of the other side of the thirteenth floor. He wanted to be a part of it and soon he would get his opportunity.

It just wasn't much of one, to start.

"The buyout was about to go down, but I didn't know what was going to happen," he said. "That fateful day, when it finally went down, as soon as we were done with the show [acting PD] Jeff K walked in. I was thinking, 'Well, at least I have my teaching certificate.'

"Jeff K told Humble that the boss wanted to see him, and Humble knew what was about to happen. I asked Jeff if the boss wanted to see me too, but he said I was good."

For the second time in his career, Lewis had dodged a bullet. But once again, he was back to the board, babysitting the new syndicated *Walton & Johnson* morning show that had taken his and Hayes' place. Dan Bennett did, however, throw Lewis a bit of a bone, saying he could occasionally sit in with *BaD Radio*.

"I'd get up early in the morning to work the board, then I'd pop in with Bob and Dan a couple of times a week—how odd was that?" Lewis said. "I'm sure they were thinking the same thing.

"Every time I was in there, I didn't say one word until I was spoken to," he said. "It was almost like they had to say, 'Well, what do you think, Donovan?' I was feeling so awkward, it was unreal. It got to the point where I told Bob and Dan I didn't know what to do and they said the same thing.

"But another month went by, and I was finally able to separate from The Bone for good," Lewis continued. "And they finally put me with Bob and Dan every day. I was still holding back, though; I didn't want to force it and screw the whole thing up. I was waiting for the game to come to me, but it wasn't coming to me because they were so used to being with each other. And I totally understood that."

What may have seemed like a smooth transition to many listeners was tearing Lewis up inside. Laying back was killing him; more important, he was in danger of watching his golden opportunity dissolve in front of his eyes. He said Sturm told him, "I know you're letting the game come to you, and that's good. But every once in a while you have to call for the ball."

The turning point finally came at Cowboys training camp of 2006, when Lewis and the rest of The Ticket hosts traveled to Oxnard, California. During this two-week trip, Lewis, Sturm and McDowell were finally able to get acquainted with each other.

"Bob suggested that I talk to Corby, because he had been in the same situation with *The Hardline*," Lewis recalled. "I picked his brain, and he said it took him a whole year to gain his confidence. And here I was barely three months into it! But Corby said, 'Be yourself. You're here for a reason.' It took my confidence from way down here to way up here.

"Those two weeks were crucial; that was the time when my airtime started increasing and my confidence grew."

Lewis knew he finally felt like he was accepted when he did an interview with actor Will Ferrell. Patrick Cranshaw, who had played Blue in *Old School*, had recently passed away, and in his honor Lewis asked Ferrell to join him in a rendition of "Dust in the Wind," just like Ferrell had done in the movie. Bob and Dan absolutely loved it, and Lewis was finally part of the show.

"I thought it was stupid, and I was going to edit it out of the interview," Lewis said. "But they loved it. I think they finally thought I could bring a little something to the show. I hadn't brought a damn thing up to that point.

"Of course I've had failed bits since then, but since then I've had the mentality that I'm going to bring something to the table every day," Lewis said. "It hurts when you fail, but that's how it is. If something is stupid, Bob and Dan are going to let you know. And you never get used to it. When you do something you think is good and they shitcan it, it doesn't feel very good."

The black thing

Of course, Lewis, Sturm and McDowell speak freely about race on the show. But that doesn't mean the talk doesn't go over the line at times. One day on the "Why Today Doesn't Suck" segment that bridges the time between *BaD Radio* and *The Hardline*, Line Four Guy said something that struck Lewis the wrong way.

"It was something totally inappropriate, and it ate at me," Lewis said. "I told Bob about it right after the fact. But he said, 'Well, you kind of position yourself as the black guy, so if someone says something about you being the black guy, you can't get upset about it.'

"Sometimes I felt that my being black was the only reason I was at The Ticket," he said. "If that had something to do with it, so be it, but I didn't want anybody [at the station] to think that was the *only* reason I was there. I don't care about other people thinking it, but I don't want the people I'm working with thinking it.

"I knew I'd paid my dues," Lewis added. "I'd been in the business since 1993, so I wasn't worried about anybody thinking I got this gig because I'm a brother. I'm black, but I'm Donovan first."

Yes, Lewis gets some, let's say, "racially tinged" e-mails from listeners, but he knows that it goes with the territory—especially considering how passionate the P1s are about nearly every topic any host brings on-air. Surprisingly, Lewis said he gets more race-centric e-mails from black listeners than white ones.

"They'll say, 'You sold out; you let those white boys say and do whatever, and you don't say a word about it.' It's unreal," Lewis said. "At first I used to get into e-mail battles, but now I just let it roll off my back. If The Ticket called any of them to take my place, they'd do it in a heartbeat."

Cool with it

Lewis made a splash early in his time at The Ticket with his "Black History Minute," which highlighted—in a humorous way, of course—somewhat obscure accomplishments by African Americans. And of course people took the segment way too seriously, claiming Lewis was making a mockery of Black History Month. "If I didn't do that, black history wouldn't be talked about at all on The Ticket," Lewis said. "But I've got to make it interesting for everyone. If you want me to read Martin Luther King, Jr.'s 'I Have a Dream' speech, that's not what we do. It's a comedy show.

"I'm proud of that, but I think I'm prouder of the 'Daily Donovan' segment," he said. "Bob and Dan don't have to rope off a segment every day, but they do. And that's fantastic."

So, after nearly twenty years spent either totally behind the scenes or as second banana on the air, is Lewis content to stay somewhat in the shadows? Or will the itch to be The Man ultimately prove too strong not to scratch?

"I'd be crazy to tell you I wouldn't want my own show one day, but right now the path is almost like I'm starting over," Lewis said. "Yeah, I've been in the business for more than fifteen years, but I haven't been on the air all the time. I've been working my way up, doing this, doing that.

"And I've finally reached the pinnacle," he said. "I may be batting ninth, but that's fine with me. I'm batting ninth on the Yankees, and I'm loving it."

Speaking of baseball, it's time to get to know a little better the guy who lives it and breathes it—and, oh yeah, who just happened to start The Ticket—Mike Rhyner.

SECTION FIVE

The Hardline

14

MIKE RHYNER

The Old Gray Wolf

"This team SUCKS."

MIKE RHYNER is The Ticket's version of Reggie Jackson: "the straw that stirs the drink." His story is the story of the birth of The Ticket. His personality on-air is part cantankerous old fart, part baseball purist and part apologist, with a rapier-like wit that's always entertaining, even when he wishes nothing but misfortune on your favorite team.

He's the kind of guy you would have loved to have as an uncle growing up, the kind who might sneak you a taste of his Crown and Coke.

But what was Rhyner himself like as a kid in Dallas' Oak Cliff section of town? About as non an entity as imaginable.

"I was not what you would call goal-oriented, but back then that term hadn't even been defined," he said. "Did I catch hell because of it? Sure. My parents thought something was off with me, but they didn't know what to call it or how to categorize it.

"And all the schools I went to were big—especially Kimball," he said. "You had to do something or have some talent or ability to get the attention of the teachers. That was out of reach for me.

"I was a good kid. I was not a tough kid," Rhyner went on. "There were a lot of tough kids around, but I was certainly not one of those. And if you weren't one, you tried to stay out of their traffic lane. That wasn't easy; you were going to have to fight, and if you weren't tough you were going to get beat up. That happened to me plenty. A lot of those guys wound up in the JD [juvenile delinquent] system."

If Rhyner took nothing else from his childhood, he took a musical inclination—specifically, the ability to play drums. While other kids were mopping floors or sacking groceries, Rhyner was gigging in bands by the time he was fifteen. And he was making some pretty damn good money, especially by 1965 standards. He and his bandmates would get in a van after school let out for the weekend and then hit the road to play joints in Wichita Falls, Palestine, Tyler, Abilene, Shreveport and Durant, Oklahoma.

"My parents thought this was a folly that would pass, but as it happened, I was able to make a little money at it, and they surely liked that idea," he said. "I thought I was in pretty tall cotton. All the other guys were working at Piggly Wiggly and such, and there I was, playing in a band and doing better in about every way than them."

And that's what he continued to do for the next fifteen years. He was doing just fine, playing five or six nights a week, either with his own groups or filling in for other musicians. But he knew full well that he was never going to be anything more than a drummer playing local gigs. And he was fine with that—for a while.

"Misspent youth, pure and simple," Rhyner said. "I was hoping that some way, somehow, it might go somewhere. But somebody's got to know how to make that happen. I didn't; nobody I ever played with or knew did. Back then, though, you could eke out a meager living doing it if you were so inclined.

"My dad and I had our ups and downs about that, for sure," he said. "He wanted me to go to Texas A&M, as he had, and had I been smart, that's what I would have done. But I was just not goal-oriented and driven like my sister. I thought I had all the answers, and I had to do my own thing."

Disco days

Rhyner was playing pretty steadily until the mid-seventies, when disco began to dominate. At that point, rock bands just weren't in demand anymore, and his gigs steadily dwindled. That's when country music came to the rescue, the same kind of music Rhyner had always dismissed as tripe for the dimwitted.

"I knew a couple of guys who had started playing country," Rhyner said. "They'd told me I should look into it, that the money was better, the gigs were better, everything about it was better. But I hated country and thought that would be a high sellout. Then one night one of them called and said he knew a guy who needed somebody in about an hour. I hadn't played in some time; I was starting to grasp the serious nature of the way things were going out there.

P1s celebrate The Hardline's *1000th show at the Corral Club at Texas Stadium.*

I thought, 'Man, how bad can it be? Don't be stupid.' I threw my drums in the car and in about an hour I was getting a crash course in country.

"The singer or the bass player would tell me before the song started how it went and what to watch for," he said. "I didn't know any of these guys, but the next week I got a call from somebody else that I didn't know, and I went and played with them a couple of nights. In no time at all I was doing three or four nights [a week], a different place and different band every night, and that later turned into five, six or even seven nights a week if I wanted to. And it was everything the guy had said—better gigs, better money. I learned that country was like any other form of music: it had its good and its not-so-good, and the trick was to be able to tell the difference."

Can you see Rhyner in a rhinestone suit wearing a bolo tie with his afro squeezed into a ten-gallon hat? It wasn't that bad, but... "I did have to wear a hat for one band, and it was awful."

Time for a change

Again, Rhyner was doing OK. He was playing enough gigs to pay the bills and give him a comfortable little life. But he was also nearing the age of thirty, and he knew it was probably time to grow up. In one of those moments nearly everyone faces at some point, Rhyner looked around and asked himself, "What the hell am I doing?" He knew the time was now to change his path, and he made a decision that would one day result in the birth of The Ticket.

"I started thinking, 'You're not just out of college or anything like that. In fact, you haven't even finished college. What's something you can do that you think you can get good at quick?' I thought of radio.

"It helped that I was somewhat of a radio maven as a kid," he said. "While all my friends were watching *My Mother the Car*, I was listening to Russ Knight the Weird Beard on KLIF. I don't know, there was just something magical about it. Something about it grabbed me.

"I fully get the one-on-one thing we have with our listeners, because I was on the other end of that," he added. "I was a KLIF P1. But it never even occurred to me that I would make a living in radio one day."

Rhyner took some radio classes at the University of Texas at Arlington, but he didn't fully get the fever for making a career in radio until he heard that KZEW (The Zoo) was looking for a news intern. The news director probably would have hired a German shepherd if it had happened to walk through the door at the right time, but it was Rhyner's good fortune that he walked through first. Without an interview Rhyner got the job, and he officially started his radio career in 1979 at the age of twenty-nine.

And he couldn't get enough.

"I was still playing country and knee-deep in school, but any time I wasn't in school or playing I was at The Zoo," Rhyner said. "I loved it. I was like a puppy dog, following around on everybody's heels, talking to everybody about what they did."

Basically, being a pain in the ass. But he couldn't have cared less.

Rhyner became friendly with The Zoo's program director, Tom Owens. Owens took to Rhyner and eventually made him his assistant. No longer a news intern, Rhyner was being groomed to be a PD himself, learning the programming side of radio. "I was headed down that road for a while," Rhyner said. "If I'd stayed with that side of the business, I'd be doing what Cat is doing."

But he knew he didn't really want to travel down that road, because he wanted to do sports. He was at the wrong station to do that, however, and he knew it. He was either going to have to create his own position at The Zoo or head somewhere else down the dial.

Then the break came, a natural one in hindsight. And it's all because the morning drive hosts, LaBella and Rody, couldn't stand sports.

"Every year they would freak out when the Cowboys started up," Rhyner said. "They'd look at each other like, 'God, what are we going to do about this?'

"They came to me one day and said, 'Why don't you start doing some stuff with us and let's see where it goes?'" he said. "I was terrible; I was nervous and I had shake-voice. I had no business being on the air—it was like Phil the intern being on the air.

"But I never came close to saying screw it. I was going to sally forth and get good at it as long as they would have me," Rhyner added. "*They* were pretty close to saying screw it, but they didn't."

He just decided to get better and he did, remaining at The Zoo as a sports reporter and show producer. If he hadn't improved he would have been canned, and there's a good chance there would have been no such thing as The Ticket.

But he did improve. However, The Zoo disappeared in 1986 and Rhyner went to WBAP, where he was the self-described "third wheel" in the sports department. He stayed there for a year and then found himself out of radio, working for On Call, a telephone information branch of GTE that provided sports news and information to GTE customers.

It was then he had another "What the hell?" moment of self-reflection. "Actually, I had lots of those then," he said. "No particular one stands out. I didn't have a bad attitude or anything like that; I got through the day-to-day of it OK. But I knew I had to do something.

"GTE treated me well, and I really liked those people, but that was a road going nowhere. I had to make something happen."

The first seeds

By 1992 Rhyner was doing an hour of sports talk a week on KAAM-AM. Nobody was listening to his show, but he didn't care. He was developing his sports-talk chops. "As I go back and listen to those shows, you can tell it's me," he said. "I'd love to think I'm a little better at it today, but as far as the 'how I do it' goes, there's not a ton of difference."

Later that year Rhyner left On Call to work full-time at KZPS-FM, once again talking sports at a station people actually listened to. "I was on the show with John LaBella, Ellen Daniels and Danny Owen," he said. "I was not expecting much, but it was a really good show, and one of the things I will always wonder about is what that might have turned into. [But] a new program director came in and scuttled the whole thing in favor of more records.

"But I would think about that show and why it was working, and gradually I saw why: we had good chemistry together," Rhyner said. "I was still going out to the ballpark and hanging out with Greggo and Junior. Seeing what happened on that show made me see them in a whole different way, and it soon became apparent to me that there was something useful in play. The question then became what to do with it."

And what happened next is the genesis of what has become one of the most popular radio stations in America, regardless of format. But that story you've already read.

Next is the story of arguably The Ticket's most unlikely star, Corby Davidson.

15

CORBY DAVIDSON

Snake

"Hey! Dill!?"

NOT EVERYONE IS A HUGE FAN of Corby Davidson. He is variously considered to be abrasive, too cool for school, a music snob and a pompous punk who's bringing down *The Hardline*. It's only natural that some people would have those opinions; after all, "The Cobra" has been surrounded by beautiful women all of his life and only drinks the finest vodka.

But the bottom line is the creator of characters like The Overcusser, Repro Man and Redundant Man has helped The Ticket's afternoon drive-time show maintain—and even exceed—the ratings established when Greg Williams was riding shotgun with Mike Rhyner.

Rhyner's introduction of Davidson's "Entertainment News for You" segment isn't complete shtick. Davidson *is* polarizing. Richie Whitt of the *Dallas Observer* wrote several articles on Williams' departure from The Ticket. The articles appear on the paper's Unfair Park blog, and at the bottom of each, several listeners posted their opinions on just what they think of the job Davidson has done since Williams left.

Here are some samples—typos, misspellings and all:

"The kid from deliverance kissing Rhyner's a$$ for four hours...anyone else here that loud sucking noise from 3-7 daily...gimme a break" Rufus

"I'm lying in my hospitol bed recooperating from the ass-whippings Corby's been administring! The nurse sadly informs me there's not enough antibiotics in Mayo clinic to heal these blisters!" d-head dave

"Expect a Line-Up change soon! Rhyner and Corby CANNOT sustain Afternoon Drive with their lame act." wreck

"korby sucks. he has the "over cusser" and repro man. that's it, nothing else. his e-news stories come from hollywood web sites and are weak. his vocabulary is lacking. he frequently re-uses words he just learned from ryner." Rick

"I like Corby as a yuk, but not as a mainstay. I don't care for drunken frat boy rhetoric in such large doses. Danny is a douche bag, but is useful in very limited instances. Mike has asked for specifics on why some feel the show is in decline. It is because Mike Rhyner is noticeably less enthusiastic about his job, it has been evident for several months now. He has ceded the show to Corby and Danny's too hip attitude. It ain't hard no more, it's a frat house. The drive time show is headed the way of Russ Martin with co douches Davidson and Bayles driving the show now. So Long Hardline, you are missed." Johnson County Bastard

"I don't know if the marginalization of Greggo over the past couple of years was his own doing or the insipid decision to give Corby/Danny more on-air time. What I do know is that Greggo was good and Corby/Danny are awful - and, I say this as a season-ticket holding OU football fan, Corbites. The Hardline has degenerated into nothing more than segments of Corby, Danny, and Mike discussing the crappy local music scene. They all suck. All of them. They suck. The Dallas music scene sucks. The people who pretend it is important and worthwhile suck." Kevin

And those were some of the nicer ones.

"That stuff doesn't bother me," Davidson said. "No matter who you are in this business you're going to have people who don't like you. It doesn't matter if you're Bob Costas or anybody else. I remember the first negative e-mail I got; they really laid into me. I was like, 'Holy shit.' I was shaking while I was reading it.

"But Mike said, 'You've got it down.' It was maybe the year I started working with him. He said, 'Fifty percent of the people really like you, and fifty percent of them can't stand you. That's what you want. Look at Howard Cosell; he was the most hated broadcaster and he was [also] the most revered.' I go, 'But I don't want to be hated.'

"He goes, 'Forget it. It's too late.'

"People who blog, or respond to blogs, are angry people," Davidson said. "They wanted answers that we weren't giving them as to why Greggo left, so they were pissed off. They're not going to be happy with anything going on with *The Hardline*. And I don't care.

"I go by the ratings, and the ratings are huge," he said. "They haven't dropped one bit since Greggo left. We're still the highest-rated show on the station, and have been since he left. I don't pay any mind to it.

"If you go to an event like Ticketstock or a big roadshow, you see how many people give you compliments," Davidson added. "I was jogging one time and the mailman came up to me and said, 'I wanted you to know what a great job you're doing.'

"You're going to get the hate e-mails, but you get way more positive feedback."

From nowhere

Whether you like him or hate him, Davidson has earned his Ticket notoriety.

Davidson was born in Fort Worth and grew up in Arlington. As a child he thought he'd be the next great Wishbone quarterback at Oklahoma, but he gave up that idea when he realized he was slower than cold tar. Then he figured he'd be a pro golfer because he was excellent in high school. But a six-inch growth spurt his junior year ruined his swing and scotched that idea.

Being a lightning rod on an all-sports radio station wasn't part of the equation.

"I never thought once about being in broadcasting—if you call what we do broadcasting," Davidson said. "It never entered my mind."

What did enter his mind was the feeling of failure. Davidson was attending the University of North Texas, but he was in his mid-twenties. While his friends were beginning their "real" careers, Davidson was waiting tables at J. Pepe's Mexican Restaurant, picking up plates of half-eaten tamales and getting stoned after work.

"I was half-assing it," Davidson said. "I had no clue about what I wanted to do. That was back in my heavy pot smoking days."

One day everything came to a head. "I had just smoked a joint and was sitting in the car wondering what the fuck I was going to do," he said. "I started to cry. There was nothing I wanted to do—nothing. Then The Ticket started up. Everybody I listened to on The Ticket sounded like they were having a really good time. It sounded like a lot of fun, and I knew a lot about sports.

"I figured, 'Why not go over there and see if they have something?'

In October 1994, Davidson approached then-assistant program director Jeff Catlin, whom he knew from high school. Catlin suggested he do an internship at the station, so Davidson did. Three months later Davidson was hired for just about the worst job there is at The Ticket, or any other radio station: weekend overnight board operator. He worked the 10 P.M. to 6 A.M. shift on Fridays and Saturdays.

The job sucked, but it may have been the biggest break of his life.

"I had no idea where I was headed at The Ticket, but I knew I had my foot in the door," Davidson said. "Once that happens, everyone will tell you it's just a matter of showing people what you can do.

"The only problem was working 10–6 on the weekends," he said. "During the week I would show up if they needed me for something, but during my regular shift I was the only soul in the building other than the security guard. I didn't get to know anyone."

Davidson begged his boss to move him to another shift. All he was doing was running commercials during the syndicated *Sporting News Radio*, which The Ticket airs while everybody else is sleeping. He would listen to *Sporting News* and make sure the station stayed on the air, praying he'd get a call from a listener so that he'd have someone to talk to.

But he stuck it out. Nine months later he was bumped up a notch, to the Saturday–Sunday 6 A.M. to 2 P.M. shift. The biggest break, however, was the chance to periodically produce "real" shows during the week when the station needed him to fill in.

"I said, 'OK, I know I can produce,'" Davidson said. "About three months later they changed all the producers. It used to be they'd have one producer working two shows, then they went to one per show. About that time Chris Arnold started working at The Ticket. We got along, and when they asked Chris who he wanted as his full-time producer he picked me. I was like, 'Holy shit, this is awesome!'"

Nobody tried to talk Davidson into going on the air. He didn't think he was anywhere near to being ready anyway. Plus, he was more than happy with the little niche he had carved out for himself.

"I don't know how to describe it other than to say I was happy," Davidson said. "I wasn't pushing anything. All I knew was I finally had a real job. If somebody asked me, I could say, 'I produce a radio show.' I was in; I was working full time with benefits. At that age that was all I was looking for, something I liked to do and something I knew I could be pretty good at.

"I wasn't completely embarrassed anymore, having to tell people, 'Uh, I'm twenty-five and I work overnights on the weekends,'" he said.

Ready for his close-up

Davidson had been with Arnold for about six months when Arnold asked him to start contributing on-air. But it wasn't a case of Davidson being rattled from his cozy existence and forced to step up to the next level. Davidson had already contributed a little here and there, and he had started interviewing athletes in the off-beat way that would become part of his trademark.

"I knew by that time I was comfortable enough to talk on the radio," Davidson said, "to Chris, at least. And about that time is when I decided I could go into locker rooms, interview people and make it pretty entertaining. That's when I met Shaq.

"After I talked to him the first time, I knew this could be a freaking goldmine," he said. "Not just with him, but anybody.

"My interactions with Shaq were getting me more airtime, and the show was doing really well," Davidson continued. "I guess I

Corby and Chris Arnold.

was developing a little bit of personality on the air, but still, I never wanted to be an on-air guy. If somebody wanted me to do that, that was fine. But I was never going to push it to the point where I was going to be that kind of guy who just has to move up the ladder."

Like it or not, though, Davidson was about to jump up a couple of rungs. Arnold, who was also the sports director at KKDA-FM (K104) as well as a television sideline reporter and master of ceremonies for Dallas Mavericks home games, left The Ticket when his work schedule became too much to maintain. He resigned abruptly, leaving Davidson in limbo.

And Davidson was pissed.

"I went to his house, and we got into it," Davidson said. "I didn't know he had resigned. I wouldn't have been mad if he had told me, but come on. I mean, we had worked together for four years.

"I thought I was done," he said.

But he wasn't. Then-program director Bruce Gilbert told him they wanted to keep him around, they just didn't know in what capacity. So for the time being, Davidson would produce the first two hours of *BaD Radio*, which would expand to a five-hour show, from 10–3.

"Dan [McDowell] called me and said he wanted me to work with them," Davidson said. "Not just producing; they wanted me to be on the air. I went in and talked to Bruce and he said it was a good idea, that it would be a role where I could thrive. Maybe I could do what Gordon Keith did.

"Now I was officially an on-air guy," he said. "I had to step it up a notch and figure out what my role would be."

Wolf's prey

So Davidson was basically thrown to the wolves. But that was fine; he was just glad he still had a job. He kept thinking that ultimately the station management would find someone to replace him on *BaD Radio* and he'd go back behind the scenes, but it never happened.

There was a change coming, however, and Davidson didn't like it at all. The Old Grey Wolf was lurking.

"I worked with Bob and Dan for six months and loved it," Davidson said. "Those guys were full of ideas and raring to go. It was awesome. I came up with 'E-News' the first day and would do it three times a show. They gave me *carte blanche* to do whatever I wanted—whether it was sports-related or not—and ratings were good.

"About that time was when the rumors of Norm coming to the station were really heating up," he said. "Bruce called me in one day and said he had an opportunity. *The Hardline* was interested in me. I'd be doing the same thing I was doing for Bob and Dan. He said he wanted to gauge whether or not I was interested, and I told him I wasn't.

"He asked me, 'So, if you had your choice, who would you choose?' I said, 'Bob and Dan. I don't know how much plainer I can make it.' Then he asked me why.

"Mike and I didn't really get along that well," Davidson said. "He was just kind of an ass to me; but he's kind of an ass to everybody until he gets to know you. He'd try to show me up sometimes during the mix and mingle, making snide little comments. And he did it off the air also.

"So I got him in a room one time and said, 'What's the fucking deal with me and you? This is bullshit. You slay me on the air, and I don't know why. I think we're alike in a lot of ways, and you're a guy I've looked up to for a while. I'd appreciate it if you'd stop.'

"He said he would, and he did," Davidson said.

Back to the discussion between Davidson and Gilbert over his on-air future. Gilbert basically laid down the law and said he didn't have an option. The chemistry between *The Hardline* and Gordon Keith had evaporated, so Keith was moving to *Dunham & Miller*. And Rhyner wanted Davidson to join him and Williams.

Case closed—the Wolf had successfully landed his prey.

"It didn't take long before I completely changed my tune working with those two guys," Davidson said. "Bob and Dan figured it would happen when they heard Norm was going to be hired; they knew they'd be back to doing three hours and didn't think there was enough time to do what they wanted with me. But they were still pissed.

"I thanked them for giving me the shot," he said. "Without them, and without Chris, both taking a chance on me, there's no way I'd be doing what I'm doing today."

It wasn't as if the transition to *The Hardline* was a smooth one, however. Davidson said it took him a year before he even began to figure out what his role would be. "I didn't have one to start," he said. "Mike was like, 'Do whatever you want to do.' They weren't extremely trustworthy of me, and I wasn't on the air much.

"I was basically replacing Gordon, who people loved," Davidson said. "I'm the guy taking over for the guy everybody thinks is the funniest human being on the planet? Good luck with all of that. But it's not about funny; it's about being entertaining. If you find something funny, great. But whatever you do, make sure it's entertaining."

Rhyner and Williams didn't exactly help Davidson find his stride. "There was really no guidance other than 'Do whatever you want—and be good,' Davidson said. "The characters I created [like Overcusser, Repro Man and Redundant Man] were a big hit, so it got me in good graces with a lot of people up there."

After about three years, Davidson got to the point where he was more or less on equal footing with Rhyner and Williams. But there was never a moment where he fully realized he was "in."

"The bottom line is, although it's a sports station, on a good day it's only half sports talk," Davidson said. "On a normal day it's about a third sports. There's just not enough going on.

"The Musers will talk Mavs at 6:10 and 6:30, and then again at 7:50 and 8:10, because they know nobody's listening for four hours," he said. "*The Hardline* didn't work that way; it was a one-shot deal. They'd talk about it and then they were done.

"It left giant holes in the show that needed to be filled," Davidson added. "I was the giant hole."

Shaq Daddy

Although Davidson had first established his penchant for silly-ass sports interviews on Chris Arnold's show, it wasn't until he joined *The Hardline* that they really flourished. Of course, the interview that made it a staple was with Shaquille O'Neal. Any time the Lakers or Heat came to Dallas, Davidson's talk with Shaq was can't-miss radio the next day.

The best question? Maybe it was when Davidson asked Shaq, "What's bigger, [5'3" point guard] Earl Boykins or your penis?"

Shaq fired back without hesitation, "Earl Boykins *is* my penis."

"The first time I talked to Shaq I was kind of nervous; I just thought it would be really funny to ask him goofy questions," Davidson said. "It was probably because I listen to Howard Stern a lot, and I remembered the type of questions Stuttering John would ask celebrities. I wouldn't ask totally offensive questions like he does, though.

"But the thing that sticks out in my mind the most about Shaq was when Miami played Dallas in the 2006 finals," he said. "It was in a big media room; about 150 people were in there. I was standing behind a huge speaker so he couldn't see me, and I asked

Corby with Rhyner and Greggo.

the attendant to hand me the microphone right at the end of the Q and A.

"The mediator goes, 'Last question,' and I go, 'Shaq, over here. If a snake bit your mom right here [points just above his left breast], would you suck the venom out to win a title?'

"He said, 'No, but I would your wife,'" Davidson said. "He got up and started pointing at me like, 'I got you!'"

Shaq knows the game, plays along and has fun with it. That's because he's a bright guy. And he's somewhat of an exception in Davidson's dealings with big-time athletes.

"I've never had a guy get mad at me, because most of them don't get it when I ask goofy questions," Davidson said. "That's the beauty of it; everybody else is in on the gag, and the athlete is the punch line. Most of the time they're just numb when I approach them. I know it going in because of all the straight reporting crap I had to do in the early days. You know the guy is looking right through you.

"But a lot of them just aren't very intelligent on top of that; they don't handle the media very well and they're just susceptible to getting fucked with," he added. "It's just the nature of it."

Flying solo in the future?

Davidson has thought about what it would be like to have his own show, and said he's had offers in the past to leave the station. But he's settled in Dallas with his wife Julie and son Isaac, and he loves The Ticket—especially now that the whole Greg Williams saga has ended.

"I'm content to the point of being complacent, probably," Davidson said. "I'm not one of those people who are constantly looking to get ahead. I've been lucky with stuff falling into my lap, but I've worked for it as well.

"I think eventually something like that will probably happen, where I'll have to make a decision one way or the other," he said. "This thing will end at some point, it just will, and I'll still be at a working age when it does.

"But for now I'm just going to continue enjoying it. It's a lot more fun now that there's not that 800-pound elephant in the room dragging us down anymore."

Much more on that 800-pound elephant later, after an update on what some former Ticket hosts are up to these days.

SECTION SIX

Where Are They Now?

16

CHUCK COOPERSTEIN

CHUCK COOPERSTEIN was brought into the nurturing bosom of The Ticket to be the unquestioned "hardcore sports guy." He had little patience for the fun and yuks of other shows on the station; his mission was to focus on the Xs and Os, to be the touchstone for "real" sports talk. If you wanted to talk about the Mavericks' lack of a shooting guard, or the Rangers' lack of a quality fourth starter, Chuck was your guy.

It was that approach that would ultimately cost him his job, but he went out the way he came in—completely comfortable with his philosophy on how a sports talk show should be run. It's a philosophy he continues to embrace to this day.

Cooperstein came to The Ticket from WIP-AM in Philadelphia, where he landed after being fired from KRLD in Dallas a month prior. Skip Bayless told Cooperstein that Mike Rhyner wanted him to be a part of The Ticket, and he jumped at the chance.

"There was absolutely no hesitation," Cooperstein said. "I had never wanted to leave Dallas in the first place. I'd heard rumblings that they may be doing something, but I had no idea what they were up to.

"I didn't get along that well with the program director at WIP anyway," he continued. "On the one hand, it was great fortune to have the opportunity there, but on the other hand, it was a great lesson. The program director tried to change me, and I didn't appreciate that. I wasn't going to give up the idea of being true to myself.

"When I left he said, 'Good luck. [The Ticket]'s never going to make it,'" Cooperstein said. "This was a guy who claimed to know Dallas radio. But WIP did give me an opportunity that I hadn't had before, a daily talk show, and it was a tremendous experience I wouldn't have traded for anything."

Cooperstein arrived in Dallas on Thanksgiving weekend of 1993. But considering the extremely uncertain beginnings of the station, it would be understandable if he was having second thoughts about his decision to leave Philadelphia.

"Maybe I was just incredibly naïve, but I always felt it was going to get done," Cooperstein said. "I was not privy to the most sensitive of the talks with investors; Mike and Skip were our liaisons. But after a month of it not happening, yeah, we were getting a little frustrated."

Everybody was trying to keep news of the nascent station on the down-low, almost to the point of paranoia. It got to the point that when it was time for the would-be show hosts to get together to discuss station developments, they didn't call it a "meeting." It was referred to as a "swordfish moment."

"It was the secret code; whenever we all wanted to get together and talk about something without letting the outside world know, it was a 'swordfish moment,'" Cooperstein said. "Greggo coined the term. These 'swordfish moments' occurred from six months before the station started to six months into it. Any time we felt there was stuff we needed to talk about that other people on the periphery didn't need to know, that would be a 'swordfish moment.' I have no idea what the purpose of the name was."

When the station finally started, Cooperstein said there was a feeling of elation permeating through the entire staff. But he'll remember the first day more for the technical meltdowns than his feeling of pride.

"It was great that we were doing something that should have been in Dallas a long time before, and I was proud to be a part of it," Cooperstein said. "But it was hard to get a feel for what the presentations were like the first week, because there were so many technical problems.

"We were doing our shows from the Super Bowl in Atlanta, and we had an engineer who was really not capable of remote engineering," he said. "But for the most part, we were on the air, and we were giving people something they hadn't had before."

Once the station had been on the air a few weeks, Cooperstein said that while he was more than comfortable with the way he was running his show, he wasn't so sure about most of the other guys.

"We were all developing our own style," Cooperstein said. "Skip was Skip, and I was definitely me. Good or bad, I was who I was. Dunham and Miller and The Hardline hadn't really done their own shows before, and it took them some time to find themselves. But their personalities—especially Greggo, because of how he sounded—were becoming very identifiable.

"I don't necessarily know that my presentation evolved all that much, because I knew exactly what I wanted to do and what I wanted my show to be," he said. "I wanted it to be a 'town square' of sports, where we were going to talk about all of it—all of it except the three things I said I'd never talk about: fantasy football, professional wrestling and high schools.

"That's what I always wanted to do, and what I believed a talk show should be. To this day I believe that's what a talk show should be."

His unflinching approach to sports talk caused him some consternation when he heard *Dunham & Miller* and *The Hardline*. Where he was hardcore, they were "guy talk."

"Sure, I had issues when the other guys went off the sports track," Cooperstein said. "That's why I got fired. [New Ticket program director] Mike "The Laddy" was a protégé of my boss in Philadelphia. He wanted me to lighten things up, and I tried to from time to time.

"But it was never about me," he said. "I wanted people to respect my opinions, but the games, how they were played and the people in the games were far more important to me. They were far more important than what restaurant I went to last night, what movie I saw or what my kids were doing. And I still believe that."

Cooperstein didn't always have the straight-up sports talk blinders on, however. In 1996 he made a bet with his audience that if then-Rangers pitcher Roger Pavlik made the All-Star team, he'd do an hour of his show standing on his head. At the time Pavlik had an 11–2 record, but his ERA was more than 5, and Cooperstein was convinced American League manager Mike Hargrove would agree with him that Pavlik didn't deserve a spot. When the news reached Cooperstein, it's safe to say it helped put a damper on his vacation in Hilton Head, South Carolina.

"Lo and behold, when the reserves and pitchers were announced, he was on the team," Cooperstein said. "I let out a scream that had to have awakened everybody in the next room. I couldn't believe I was going to have to do it.

"Anyway, the Monday after I got back from vacation I did the last hour of the show on an inversion table," he said. "I sat up during the breaks—you can't be on your head for an hour, it's just not healthy. But we turned the monitor upside down so I could see who was calling. It really was a funny deal."

One that happened far too infrequently on Cooperstein's show for The Laddy's tastes.

Out of the blue

Cooperstein was perfectly content, confident he was doing the kind of show that was not only right for him, but right for The Ticket as well. However, The Laddy didn't feel the same way, and he called Cooperstein in his office one day in June 1997 to deliver the stunning news to "The Higher Authority."

"He called me in to tell me I was fired, and it came totally out of left field," Cooperstein said. "I thought he was going to tell me my contract was being extended; after all, my ratings were great.

"I had been switched from 4–7 [to the 10–noon time slot] and I was upset about that, but I got over it," Cooperstein said. "The only thing it really hurt was my golf.

"But I was doing great in the time slot," he went on. "I had gotten great interviews; I had just had Wilt Chamberlain on for an hour, and I had Michael Irvin during the midst of his craziness. We had some really good stuff. But it wasn't what they wanted.

"As it turns out, they ultimately realized they made a mistake, because they eventually moved Norm over," Cooperstein said. "They knew they had to have someone to give them some sports legitimacy."

The Laddy, while not saying he felt he made a mistake, did admit it was extremely difficult for him to make the call on Cooperstein. "My easiest decision was getting rid of Skip and moving The Musers to his time slot," The Laddy said. "But Chuck was tough—he's a good guy. The hardest thing about replacing him was that the other guys were really nervous about it. They thought he was the touchstone of sports at The Ticket, and they didn't think [letting him go] was a good idea."

Bouncing back

Cooperstein didn't have to wait long to get back into the business after leaving The Ticket, as WBAP quickly picked him up to perform his brand of sports talk nightly after Randy Galloway's show. His did his 8 P.M. to midnight show for three and a half years before moving with Galloway to ESPN Radio. He no longer does a daily talk show but serves as the radio voice of the Dallas Mavericks.

While Cooperstein still doesn't understand the decision The Laddy made, he can at least laugh about it, and the fact that he's bounced around the Dallas dial. "I've worked a lot of places in this town," Cooperstein said. "I'm running out of places to work around here."

17

CURT MENEFEE

CURT MENEFEE has become the highest-profile ex-Ticket personality, as he is now known nationally as the host of the extremely successful Fox NFL Sunday pre-game studio show. As a Day One host, Menefee established himself as the easygoing counterpart to the ultra-abrasive Skip Bayless, who hosted the show prior to Menefee's. (Bayless declined to be interviewed for this book.)

Menefee was already well-known to Dallas-Fort Worth sports fans as the weeknight anchor for Channel 11 Sports. About three months before being contacted by Mike Rhyner to come aboard with The Ticket, Menefee was hosting his own talk show on KGBS-AM (1190) in addition to his Channel 11 duties.

"If we had two callers a day, that was great," Menefee said. "I don't know if anybody even knew it existed. It felt like I was talking to air most of the time."

Rhyner and the Channel 11 news director sat down with Menefee a few weeks later. Menefee's stint at KGBS was about to end, and he didn't have any say in the matter.

"They told me they wanted me to host the show at The Ticket, and I was like, 'Well, I just committed to this other station. I appreciate the offer, but I can't really accept it,'" Menefee said. "They said, 'No, you don't understand. We want you to work at The Ticket because this is going to be a bigger deal. If you refuse, we'll just say you don't have permission to work at the other station.'

"I was a little upset at that," he said. "That's not the way to do things; commit to somebody and then leave two or three months later. I really had no say in it, but the guys at 1190 totally understood.

"It was good, though, because I had two places that wanted me."

Once he talked in depth with Rhyner and got the details about plans for the station, Menefee started warming to the idea. He was impressed by the amount of planning and thought that had gone into it, and he had a good feeling about its chances for success.

Menefee's day job at Channel 11 was solid, so he didn't really have to sweat the uncertainty surrounding the station's unveiling like the other hosts did. "I didn't think it wasn't going to happen," he said. "I came in relatively late in the game, so I didn't have to wait as long as some of the other guys."

His memories of the first day on air are clouded in a haze of cough-and-cold medicine, although the constant dinging of a hotel elevator stands out.

"The Cowboys were playing the 49ers in the NFC Championship Game in Dallas the week before we went on air," Menefee said. "As part of my duties at Channel 11, I went out to San Francisco the week before the championship game to cover the 49ers. I stayed there until the day before the Cowboys–49ers game.

"I started feeling like I was getting a cold, but I covered the game and did the broadcast afterward, then hopped a plane for Atlanta and the Super Bowl after the Cowboys won," he said. "I was really sick by the time I got to Atlanta—the cold had turned into something else.

"Anyway, the next day was the first day of The Ticket, and I did my show by remote from the media hotel in Atlanta. I took a lot of cold medicine to try and blow this thing out of my head," Menefee said. "I remember going to do my show. I showed up maybe an hour beforehand. They were having technical issues; equipment was going in and out. We weren't sure what was going to happen, but I was hopped up on cough medicine. It wasn't that big a deal to me.

"But the equipment totally crapped out. They wanted to stay on the air, obviously, because it was their first day," he said. "And this was in the days before cell phones, so I had to do my show from a payphone. I literally had to go to a phone at the media hotel right beside the elevator at the Atlanta Hyatt Regency. Every fifteen seconds the bell was ringing for the elevator, and I was trying to sit there doing a radio show.

"I was wondering what I had gotten into."

What he had gotten himself into was a radio show that was a complete 180 from what he had been doing at 1190. He received more calls that one day than he would have fielded in an entire week at the other station. That's when he knew The Ticket was going to take off.

"You had this many people listening already, and the station was only five hours old," Menefee said. "We were wall-to-wall calls. I can't stress enough how unbelievable that was to me after having been down the dial.

"After that first day, I got to my Channel 11 duties, took some more cough syrup and went to bed," he said. "The second day, I got up to do the show and the equipment was fixed. But the producer told me I referred to The Ticket as 'AM 1190' six or seven times during the show. That wasn't a good sign, but it was just one of those things. Being hopped up on cough medicine didn't help."

Menefee likens the station's progress in those early days to the development of a child. Day One was its birth, and it went through the accompanying growing pains. As the weeks ensued, the child began to crawl. By the time Menefee left, The Ticket was old enough to take care of itself and smart enough to know what worked and what didn't. The execution wasn't necessarily there all the time, but you could see it coming together. And nobody had even the slightest inkling of how big The Ticket would become.

"We were having a blast, and the callers were having a blast," Menefee said. "Skip's show was hardcore and he ticked off a lot of people, but that was his thing. My show was more fun; we'd have 'Ticked-Off Tuesdays' where people would call in and tell us what they were mad about. That was one of the more popular things we did.

"We had one day where callers had to give me their favorite TV theme song before we talked about sports," he said. "Another day they had to give me a one-hit wonder in both sports and music, like Paco and Joe Charbonneau. We wanted to have fun in addition to talking serious sports.

"It was a knowledgeable but playful place," he added. "The callers enjoyed it because there was nothing else like it at the time. Nowhere else in Dallas could you get all-day, all-sports radio."

Time to go

Unlike most of his counterparts who left the station, Menefee's departure from The Ticket occurred without a hint of acrimony or controversy. He was the "guy who had the nice departure," as he put it.

The offer he left to accept was simply too good to refuse. His Channel 11 contract was nearing its end, and he started contemplating whether or not he wanted to pursue a job in a larger market. He received an offer from the sports director at the new Fox station, Channel 33, to be their No. 1 sports anchor. The channel was in the process of forming a completely new news operation from scratch.

But he was thinking of bigger opportunities and declined the offer. It's a good thing, because Fox eventually bought Channel 4. But Channel 4 already had a strong news operation, so management decided to scrap plans to develop the same thing at Channel 33 only days before it was supposed to start.

It just so happened that the would-be Channel 33 news director was transferred to WNYW, the Fox-owned TV station in New York

City. She knew Menefee's Channel 11 contract was just about up and wanted him to come to New York. Badly.

"It was a no-brainer, having the chance to be the number one guy on a station in the number one market," Menefee said. "It's nice to be wanted. This business is so subjective; you find somebody who likes you, and sometimes when they bounce around they bring you with them."

Menefee stayed at WNYW until 2002. He had also done NFL games for Fox in 1998 and caught the play-by-play bug, and eventually he decided he didn't want to do local news anymore. MSG Network offered him a job doing play-by-play for Brooklyn Cyclones minor league baseball and the WNBA's New York Liberty, as well as host the *Sports Desk* show, sort of MSG's version of *SportsCenter*. He would later come close to getting the play-by-play position with the expansion Charlotte Bobcats: he was one of two finalists, but he didn't get the gig.

And that's probably for the best. Even though Menefee had never entertained the possibility of being a studio host for an NFL pregame show, that opportunity presented itself when James Brown left Fox for CBS. Menefee started hosting the halftime highlights segment in 2006, then filled in as studio host for then-main host Joe Buck during the playoffs that year. He was rewarded with the full-time host slot beginning in the 2007 season.

"It wasn't even in the back of my mind," Menefee said. "I used to watch *The NFL Today* when I was a kid, with Brent Musberger, Phyllis George, Irv Cross and Jimmy the Greek, and I always thought that would be a dream job.

"But I thought JB was going to be at Fox for another twenty years, and CBS had Jim Nantz and Greg Gumbel," he said. "Those were the only two opportunities, since NBC didn't have the NFL at the time. So I didn't think it was going to happen; I thought my fortunes were going to lie in being the best play-by-play guy I could be.

"But it's funny how things work out sometimes. This is the most fun job I've had—especially with the nine-week vacations."

Although he's officially hit the Big Time, Menefee still keeps tabs on The Ticket, and still marvels at its success.

"It's amazing in that, yeah, Dallas is a great sports market, but there are a lot of great sports markets where the sports radio station isn't the dominant station in town like it is with The Ticket," Menefee said. "It's surprising from the standpoint of something like that being able to happen in this day and age.

"But on the other hand it's not surprising," he said. "I go back to my original meeting with Mike Rhyner. When he sat down with me and laid out the plans for the station, it was apparent he and everybody else had done their homework. When you're with people who know what they're getting into and know how to proceed with their plan, then you shouldn't be surprised when they succeed.

"They had a plan, and they executed it properly."

18

ROCCO PENDOLA

ROCCO PENDOLA'S TENURE at The Ticket can't be characterized as anything less than a disaster. On the abrasiveness scale, Pendola made Corby Davidson look like Mr. Rogers.

When he took over for the fired Cooperstein in 1997, Pendola was a twenty-two-year-old kid who had life by the balls. He had his own show in a Top 10 market, something guys who had been in the business thirty years would have killed for. But he was also a phenomenal prick who alienated just about everyone he came in contact with.

Fast forward more than a decade, though, and the Pendola of today has done a 180. Talk to him now and you'll find a reflective, intelligent person. In fact, you'll find it hard to believe this is the same guy who probably had you screaming at your radio from noon to three on a regular basis.

"One thing I've dealt with my whole life is depression and anxiety, and it all kind of came to a head recently," Pendola said. "I started going to therapy a couple of years ago. I kind of knew, since there's sort of a family history of it, but I hid it for a long time just because that's what people do.

"I've never really dealt with these things, which I think is part of the reason why I behaved the way I did when I was in radio," he said. "I'd been dealing with it since I was a teenager.

"I had this sort of script written out for myself—I was going to work in radio and be a number one guy," he continued. "When I stopped doing that I went to school and found I was pretty good at doing research, so I decided I was going to go after a PhD, the pinnacle of education.

"All along I'm not sure these were things I wanted to do; I just felt like they were things I 'should' be doing because I was capable of them. That's where I had a conflict with myself that I realized I had to deal with."

Pendola thought his destiny was in radio, and he put those career blinders on at the ridiculously early age of thirteen, when he got his first job. He grew up a radio fanatic in Niagara Falls, New York, first listening to Buffalo-area FM stations, then becoming enamored with sports radio because he could pick up WFAN out of New York City at night.

Pendola would incessantly call in to the morning show of a Niagara Falls station, WJJL-AM, to bash the Buffalo sports teams, becoming, he said, something of a minor local celebrity. He was asked to visit the station in person, to capitalize on the minor buzz he had created. Pendola took the opportunity to start nagging station personnel in hopes of finding some sort of job. The host of the show, Gary McNamara (who is now the co-host of the overnight *Midnight Trucking Radio Network* show on WBAP), eventually offered the barely-teenaged Pendola a job giving quarter-hour sports updates on the weekends.

That led to his own weekend talk show on the station in 1989. Four years later he went to WGR in Buffalo, where he was a producer and weekend host. He left in 1995 to do nights at WQAM-AM in Miami, then moved to WTAE-AM in Pittsburgh, where he was hired by former Ticket program director Bruce Gilbert. But, leery of the impending sale of the station, Pendola sent out some tapes to Rick Scott, a sports-radio consultant based in Washington, D.C. Scott liked what he heard and forwarded those tapes to then program director, The Laddy, who hired Pendola in the spring of 1997.

"I don't really remember how I felt at the time, but I guess I was flattered; here's this sports-radio consultant who worked with all the top sports radio stations," Pendola said. "He thought I'd be a good fit, and so did The Laddy. At twenty-two years old, I felt like I was on top of the world. I was definitely excited, and I was cocky.

"I probably had bigger aspirations, but I probably was more or less thinking I really had to kick ass to either make a lot of money in Dallas or make it to New York, Chicago or one of the really big markets," he said.

Who does this kid think he is?

The Laddy would soon move to Philadelphia, leaving Pendola with the feeling of being on his own at The Ticket. Pendola doesn't remember any specific interactions with Ticket personnel upon his arrival other than the superficial "How are you doing?" types of greetings in the cubicle area.

"Maybe people were incredibly nice to me, maybe they weren't; I don't remember either way," Pendola said. "Once I started opening my mouth on the air, that's when I remember."

Pendola was a bad fit for the station from the first day he took the air. He was brash and he knew his hockey, but far too many times he came off as a complete buffoon in other areas. But whenever he did a self-critique, he thought everything he did was right.

"I thought I was doing great, that this was why they wanted me," Pendola said. "Now I look back at Rick Scott liking me and I realize these consultants like the 'flavor of the month'; they look for what's going to be attention-grabbing at a particular moment.

"In sports radio at the time, it was all about finding the loudest,

most entertaining guy who didn't necessarily talk sports all of the time," he went on. "He may not be the most astute sports person, but he can be entertaining, he can talk about a whole bunch of different things. It was more like 'Let's grab this guy and throw him in there, because he kind of defines this "thing" that we think is good in sports radio.'

"So at the time, yeah, I felt I was kicking ass," Pendola said. "I thought I was doing a great job, doing what I was supposed to do. Being loud, getting attention, doing the kind of radio show that people react to. I would openly say that it didn't matter what other people thought at the station or elsewhere—I was doing a radio show I thought I was good, and that's why I was there. I wasn't concerned with how I was perceived or with cultivating relationships with people at the station. It just didn't matter to me then."

Pendola was an abrasive Yankee who threw all caution to the wind and couldn't give a quarter of a damn about what anybody thought—on the air or off. He thought that since he was doing a show that generated controversy, everybody at the station should be happy with him.

"Now I understand there was a better way to approach it: going in a little bit quieter and then building up," Pendola said. "The first thing should have been trying to be myself and developing relationships with people. Once they got to know me, they might have accepted some of my different quirks. That's how life is.

"But I didn't know how to do that," he said. "I didn't know how to have good social relationships with people in that situation, especially people who were older than me who I may have felt threatened by. I felt they just should have accepted me.

"My defense mechanism, I guess, was to go on the air and put up this front of being a maniac, take on that persona and forget about everything else I didn't understand or care to deal with."

Pendola said that among his fellow Ticket hosts there weren't a lot of shouting matches or other explicit signs of contempt. About the only person who really outwardly showed dislike toward him, Pendola said, was Mike Rhyner. "We would do stupid things like glare at each other in the cubicle area, just dumb stuff," Pendola said.

"Gordo was probably the most outspoken person to me off the air," Pendola added. "He wanted me to be the person on the air that he talked to off the air. That was the greatest advice I had ever gotten, but obviously I wasn't ready to accept it. Gordo and I would get into it; he was always appropriate, and my reaction—which was always the case when I didn't want to deal with something, or couldn't really understand what he was coming at me with—was to blow it off."

It was clear to everybody but Pendola that his days at The Ticket were numbered. But it took an outsider to light the fuse that led to the final explosion.

His Ticket out

In the March 18, 1999 issue of the *Dallas Observer*, Robert Wilonsky wrote a scathing indictment of Pendola. Even though it was a very small portion of a larger article titled "Talking up The Ticket," it was the impetus behind Pendola's departure from the station. Here is an excerpt from that article.

In June 1997, Cooperstein would be run off by now-ex-program director The Laddy, who felt Cooperstein's higher-authority acumen didn't fit in with the burgeoning more-comedy-less-sports format. Cooperstein eventually landed at WBAP-AM, after Randy Galloway's 6–8 P.M. so-called "wimp-free" sports show—a perfect fit.

Cooperstein's replacement, Rocco Pendola, would signal all that's so unnervingly wrong with The Ticket. Pendola might well be the most obtuse, most invidious personality on local radio, a guy who didn't graduate from high school, thinks Monty Python is one man and believes it's actually possible to donate your liver while still living. And he's the antithesis of *Dunham & Miller* and *The Hardline*: a Yankee transplant who doesn't so much talk as he barks, screams and yowls incessantly. Pendola is some New York City consultant's idea of a sports-radio afternoon host.

His colleagues aren't inclined to speak about Pendola on the record, though their treatment of him on the air says enough: Pendola is often portrayed as a moronic, screaming monkey.

Harsh? Of course. But considering the feedback readers posted to the *Oberserver*'s Unfair Park blog, Wilonsky was preaching to the choir.

A stunned Pendola saw the article the night it came out, and it hit him like a shotgun blast.

"That was a pretty bad day," Pendola said. "The depression stuff, I just kind of went through that and ignored it. When that article hit, though, that was the first thing I'd ever read about myself that really hit me hard.

"I didn't know about it when it first came out," he said. "I was friendly with a couple of guys who were on The Eagle [KEGL-FM], and when I got home from my show that day I got an e-mail from them that just said, 'Sorry, man.' I e-mailed back to ask them what they were talking about, and they said I better get a copy of the paper.

"I walked over to this little bagel place that was down the street from where I lived in Valley Ranch and picked it up," he continued. "I was floored. I remember walking around Valley Ranch reading the article, just really upset. I couldn't believe what I had just read. Part of me was angry because nobody ever called me about the article, and I was also angry because I felt somebody at the station had contributed to it.

"More than that, I was just generally upset. At that point I really started re-assessing my life and thinking to myself, 'Whether it's factual doesn't really matter. This is what people think of you. Ten years from now, is that how you want people to think of you?' I knew I had to make some profound changes in my life, but in that moment I wasn't prepared or equipped to deal with it. I didn't know what to do."

The only thing he could think of was to go scorched earth. The next day on his show, he either went on a tirade against Wilonsky or didn't make a major deal out of it, depending on who you believe. A week later the *Observer* wrote: "On Friday, [Pendola] went on the air ranting about how upset he was by the story. He claimed, among other things, that he and the article's author, Robert Wilonsky, were old friends and that Wilonsky had betrayed him. In fact, the two have met only once—for about five minutes at Dallas Cowboys training camp last August."

Pendola said he went on the air and made some "little references" to the piece, but nothing major. Whatever happened on Friday was a fart in the wind compared to what happened the next day—forty-five minutes that will forever live in Ticket infamy.

Thoroughly explaining what happened when Pendola called in to Gordon Keith's *Bohemian Rant* show would probably take another five thousand words. The short and sweet version is that Keith re-played Pendola's previous-day reaction to the article, and then Pendola called to offer a rebuttal. He basically said that Gordon and Rhyner had tried to sabotage him, and that he'd never had a chance to succeed.

As the *Observer* would later put it, "Pendola and Keith had what one die-hard Ticket fan describes on the Internet as 'a personal conversation that you really had no business hearing.' According to some who heard the exchange, Pendola ripped into Keith and, for some reason, *Hardline* co-host Mike Rhyner, claiming neither of them gave him a fair chance at the station."

By the time Pendola was finished, his Ticket career was, for all intents and purposes, over.

"I knew I had some issues, and I knew I had to work on them," Pendola said. "I knew this was a wake-up call.

"But again, in that moment, I didn't know what to do," he said. "I consciously decided—knowing it was wrong, but not knowing anything else to do—to let things blow up and see what happened. I figured the article alone had pretty much sealed my fate; I didn't think there was a chance my contract would have been renewed no matter what I would have done.

"It was that phone call where I really started digging my grave. I was like, 'Screw it.' It was one of the most embarrassing moments of my life."

Pendola was basically a dead man walking the remainder of that weekend, but he showed up at a scheduled remote from 8–10 A.M. on Monday, which was held at a 7-Eleven near the studio. He did his call-ins as planned during *Dunham & Miller*, never interacting with either host. When he arrived at the station he met with his producer, Rick Arnett. It was business as usual, although Pendola knew the axe was about to fall.

"I was just waiting; I knew there was no way I'd be able to go on the air," Pendola said. "I saw Bruce, who looked like death warmed over. He said, 'I need to talk to you in a few minutes,' and I knew what it was all about.

"He called me into his office about one and he looked like he was really sick about things," Pendola said. "We were friends; I'd go to his house on holidays when I didn't go back home. He said we couldn't go on like this, and I agreed. And that was that; it wasn't a big deal. He said they'd pay me through the rest of the contract, we talked about a few logistical things, and then I was out. That was it.

"I chopped my own head off with what I ended up doing, but even if I [hadn't done] the things that followed, I don't think it would have mattered. I felt like that article was the beginning of the end."

Gilbert compared the firing to what a pro sports team has to do when there is a distracting element in the locker room.

"That came about because it was just apparent there was bad chemistry," Gilbert said. "One of the things that made The Ticket work was it was a 'good clubhouse.' Everybody knew each other, everybody got along, and Rocco had a problem with that.

"I'm not speaking out of school, and Rocco and I are good friends today, but it just wasn't a good match," Gilbert added. "They didn't play well together, for whatever the reason. There was plenty of blame to go around, but it was clear that he wasn't the right guy for the room."

So it was time for Pendola to exit that room and proceed head-long into an uncertain future.

Growing up—fast

Pendola had to try to sort out his personal issues while at the same time trying to find another job. All he knew was radio, so he took a job with the now-defunct SportsFan Radio Network in Las Vegas, a city he characterized as a "brutal place to live." But the job would lead to a self-realization.

"The good thing was the show was from six to ten in the morning, so I had all day to think," Pendola said. "They flew me to Boston for the 1999 All-Star Game. I'd never been to that kind of a big city before; I spent four days there, and I loved it. The closest thing to Boston was San Francisco, and I liked the weather better in San Francisco, so I decided to drop everything and go. It was the first out-of-character thing I'd ever done."

He worked part time at a rock radio station while also working a job selling sports hospitality packages. "I was cold-calling big companies all day; it was the kind of job you'd see in *Boiler Room* or *Glengarry Glen Ross*, but it was a good time to have a job like that," Pendola said. "It was during the dot-com boom, when everybody in Silicon Valley was spending money like it was going out of style. I did really well for a couple of years.

"I was content doing that and met a lot of great people," he said. "Then 9/11 happened and it was another one of those times that made me re-assess things and ask myself where I was going in life. I kind of revisited the same old issues from Dallas—the whole Dallas thing had never left me and it really still hasn't. It's still something I think about."

Pendola had saved enough money from his sales job to finally pursue the college degree he had ignored. He had developed a love for the different kinds of cities found in America, so he decided to major in urban studies at San Francisco State. During what he characterizes as the best four years of his life, he got married, his daughter was born and he decided to pursue a PhD.

"I didn't even know what that really was, other than some letters after my name, but I had started really getting into research," Pendola said. "I published an article and a professor suggested I pursue it, and it made sense to me."

But his depression and anxiety never left him, and he put the PhD on hold to once again figure out what he really wanted to do. He addressed his problem by starting to go to therapy in 2006, and he is currently living in Irvine, located between Los Angeles and San Diego.

"Right now I'm not doing anything, but I plan on doing something soon," Pendola said. "It could be as a bicycle messenger; it could be anything. There are a lot of television networks out here, obviously, so I wouldn't mind doing something having to do with research. Behind-the-scenes kind of stuff.

"I just want to do what I want to do," he said. "I don't want to do radio anymore, because that's what I was 'supposed' to do. I'm done telling myself what I'm 'supposed' to do. If I end up riding around downtown L.A. on a bicycle, so be it."

A good thing?

This isn't meant to be one of those touchy-feely, warm-fuzzy kinds of stories where the hot-headed young kid realizes the error of his ways and becomes a model citizen. Pendola still struggles with his affliction on a daily basis, and maybe always will.

But he acknowledges that the portion of Wilonsky's article that rocked his world forced him to re-evaluate exactly who he was and what kind of effect he'd been having on other people. It compelled him to mature.

So, in retrospect, as devastating as it was for him to read and accept, the article may have actually ended up having a positive affect on Pendola.

"It totally helped me," Pendola said. "Another thing that happened at that time was that Gordo told me something to the effect that all I cared about was radio, and there was a lot more to life. He said, 'One day something is going to happen in your life, and you're going to realize that. You're going to find out there's a big, huge world out there, and you're going to want to seek out knowledge and what the world has to offer. You'll have an unquenchable thirst for it.'

"Of course, at the time I probably said 'Fuck you' or whatever, reacting like I normally would because I couldn't handle thinking in those terms. At the time it meant nothing; but looking back, the article and what he said to me were definitely bad things at the moment, but incredibly positive in terms of shaping the direction I've gone. Not necessarily in terms of what I've done, but in the ways I've thought about myself, who I want to be, and how I want to handle my relationships with other people.

"In some ways I'm at peace," Pendola said. "I think and talk about a lot of things that I never used to consider, which is good. There are some things that still aren't evolved, but that's life.

"I think a lot about whether or not I'm doing a good enough job as a parent. I don't want to damage my kid in any way. Springsteen has a great line in one of his newer songs where he says something like, 'If I had one wish in the godforsaken world, kid, it would be that your sins would be your own.'

"I look at myself and think of the influences my parents had on me—some good, some bad—and I don't want any of my faults or quirks being the basis of any problems my daughter may have when she gets older."

19

CHRIS ARNOLD

CHRIS ARNOLD was "all that and a bag of chips" during his nearly five years at The Ticket. His velvet-smooth, laid-back delivery was a staple during the ten to noon time slot, consistently driving strong ratings.

But although Arnold's on-air persona was easygoing, in reality he was the hardest-working man in Dallas sports media. At one time, Arnold worked at K104, The Ticket and Channel 8, and did sideline reports during Dallas Maverick game broadcasts. Although nobody knew it at the time, the schedule was driving him crazy. Something had to give.

Welcome to the family

Arnold started working at K104 in 1980—long before The Ticket was even a gleam in Mike Rhyner's eye. K104 was a ratings power-house; when Curt Menefee left The Ticket for New York in 1995, hardly any consideration was given to bringing Arnold over to take his place. But luck and timing combined to make it happen.

"I'd known Rhyner, Hammer, Craig and George forever, and I knew they were going to start up a station," Arnold said. "They didn't know I knew, but I knew. I knew some of the people they were talking to, but I wasn't going to tell anybody anything. And I had no plans to be a part of it.

"Well, I was in between negotiating contracts at K104, and because of that little loophole, I had the opportunity to work at The Ticket as well," he said. "I didn't want to leave K104; we had a dynasty in the making. We knew we had lightning in a bottle. *Skip Murphy & Company* [the show on which Arnold did sports each weekday morning] was number one in every single demographic for three straight years, and the station as a whole was number one for six straight years.

"Mike never knew there was a possibility of me working at The Ticket, but we talked about it and thought it would be a great thing," Arnold said. "If Tom Joyner could work a show in Dallas and Chicago every day, I definitely could drive across town to do another one."

It was a no-brainer. Arnold's show would air right after his K104 show ended. On The Ticket, he'd be sandwiched in between Skip Bayless and *The Hardline*. He'd bring some of his K104 fans over with him without making a huge dent in the behemoth's ratings, while at the same time bumping up those of The Little Ticket.

The only real concern was how he'd manage to get to his Ticket show on time, since he had to haul ass from Grand Prairie to near Mockingbird Lane and Central Expressway.

"It was an adventure every day," Arnold said. "It was a twenty-minute drive in normal traffic, and I couldn't afford to be late. I had the Traffic Central guys on speed dial.

"Everybody was always worried about whether or not I could make it, but I was only late twice in five years," he said. "Corby [Davidson, his then-producer] and I would do our show prep for the next day after we went off the air, then I'd tweak it the next morning at 104. I'd usually hit the studio five or ten minutes before I had to go on the air."

Arnold was everywhere a major sporting event took place—Final Fours, World Series, Super Bowls, Olympics, major boxing bouts, you name it. K104 had sent him across the country, and he had the contacts that would bring him instant credibility as a Ticket host.

"I had the sports rolodex—nobody had the contacts that I had in Dallas-Fort Worth, and I don't think anybody does to this day," Arnold said. "The reason I had these contacts and could get people on my show is I would go to all the games and talk to players and coaches in the locker room. It was first-person knowledge, not just 'I caught something on TV and here's my opinion on it.'

"For years, Troy Aikman wouldn't go on The Ticket except for my show because Bayless was on," he said. "Even after Skip left, he'd still have nothing to do with The Ticket. Cowboys officials were amazed that he did my show."

Arnold himself was often amazed he could do his own show, especially during the many road trips he took for K104. One year in Cleveland he did a Ticket show from the Rock and Roll Hall of Fame. Another time he did one from the Radio Hall of Fame in Chicago, where he was covering the NBA Finals. Yet another time he did one from Rush Limbaugh's studio in New York. He even did a show from a Las Vegas casino lounge, since he was in town covering a fight.

And sometimes signals were scrambled between Dallas and wherever Arnold was broadcasting from. When that occurred, Arnold and Davidson had to improvise.

"One year I was covering a fight in Atlantic City and Corby was with me," Arnold said. "There was a miscommunication on how the show was supposed to be set up. We had the telecommunications line but no equipment, because the people at the studio in Atlantic City thought we were going to bring our own.

"Now, we're no engineers, but we saw somebody else's equipment sitting in the corner," he said. "Corby talked to our engineer in Dallas, and he put it together with bailing wire and duct tape. We had no idea whose equipment it was to even ask to use it, so we just stole it. Hey, it was just sitting there!

"When the guy showed up and we explained what we did, he went ballistic," Arnold said. "He ended up sending The Ticket a bill for a couple grand."

Keeping everybody happy

At first K104 management wasn't thrilled with the idea of Arnold working at The Ticket, but his morning show co-hosts Murphy and Nannette Lee liked the idea. That support, Arnold said, was the reason he was able to do the show.

"I wouldn't have been able to do it if they hadn't been on board," Arnold said. "They thought it would be a great way to cross-promote. I told management that this wasn't going to hurt 104. It's AM versus FM, sports versus music, and it wasn't going to hurt my performance."

But the pressure was on Arnold to make sure he didn't give anybody at K104, or Channel 8 for that matter, any reason to get rid of him. One way he did that was to make sure all of his employers had equal access to any high-profile interviews. Case in point was his exclusive talk with former Maverick Roy Tarpley, whose career was derailed by drugs.

"I worked hard to make sure everybody was happy," Arnold said. "The first big interview I had on The Ticket was Tarpley. He hadn't talked to anybody, and this was right after he'd failed a drug test and was banned from the NBA.

"But I got the interview with him on [both] 104 and The Ticket, and had a sit-down interview from his house for Channel 8," he said. "I covered all the bases; I didn't want anybody mad that I didn't take care of them. I was serving three masters at the time, and I didn't want anybody to feel like they were being slighted.

"If I had somebody big for The Ticket, I'd check with K104 to see if they wanted them, too," Arnold said. "Most of the time they didn't because they didn't devote a lot of time to sports. I never had any problems from The Ticket. Back then it was The Little Ticket; we were just lucky to be on the air."

If juggling three jobs wasn't hard enough, Arnold decided to add the Dallas Mavericks to his list of employers, filling in for Dallas-Fort Worth radio legend Kevin McCarthy as the Mavericks' public address announcer when McCarthy was having health problems. It actually ended up spawning a funny Ticket bit. The next day on *The Hardline*, "secret audio" surfaced of the Fake Chris Arnold (FCA) doing PA at that Mavs game, explaining McCarthy's absence.

"Kevin's not feeling well tonight because he had a little too much to eat," FCA said. "He had some Twinkies, two vanilla milkshakes and a Salllllllsbury steak. He had all that and a bag of chips."

OK, so maybe it doesn't translate so well to print. But on radio it was funny as hell.

Anyway . . .McCarthy ended up missing the rest of the season, so Arnold finished it for him. The Mavericks hired Arnold as a sideline reporter for TV broadcasts starting in the spring of 1996.

"It was crazy," Arnold said. "How I did it, I don't know. Back then I just had a lot of energy. I stayed in shape, worked out a lot, and basically didn't have any other life except sports."

Holding three jobs at one time is crazy; four is insane. Arnold would soon have to decide—not whether or not to give up The Ticket, but which TV job he would drop, Channel 8 or the Mavs' broadcasts.

Michael Jordan helped him make that call.

"Michael complimented me before a Bulls–Mavericks game one night about my sideline work, and it made me think," Arnold said. "I asked him 'How do you know about that?' He said, 'I have satellite; I'm checking you out all the time.'

"I put that in perspective. Channel 8 was great, but it was local," he said. "The Mavericks were sorry, so there weren't a lot of people watching them. When people saw me around town they'd say, 'You do a great job with K104 or The Ticket or Channel 8.' I was never getting any Mavs feedback, except from the organization.

"But when Jordan told me he watched me on satellite, I said 'Wait a minute,'" Arnold said. "This Mavericks thing is bigger than Channel 8. So I decided to stay with the Mavs and phase out Channel 8."

The Jordan remark wasn't simply random happenstance. Jordan knew Arnold, just like seemingly everybody else in the sports world did. During that Bulls shoot-around at Reunion Arena, Jordan, Scottie Pippen and Dennis Rodman all agreed to talk to him. They wouldn't have done that for just anybody.

"I'm not going to say I'm the Jackie Robinson of electronic media, but I've been around a long time," Arnold said. "I talk to athletes about more than just the game. Plus, back then there weren't as many reporters hanging around. But I'd talk to them about more than scoring thirty points or scoring a touchdown. I'd also run into them at functions, like fundraising events and golf tournaments, and I'd make it a point to talk to them.

"I never treated them like I was in awe of them; I treat them like regular guys and they remember that," he said. "I'd see MJ at a fight or in a casino and start shooting the bull with him. I'd develop relationships beyond that of just being a reporter.

"And, again, I'd go to all of the games. If I walk into a locker room and Shaq says, 'Chris, what's going on, man?' the younger guys see I have a relationship with him and they figure I must be cool.

"In fact, I introduced Shaq to Corby," he added. "I told Shaq, 'He's cool. He's going to ask you some different kinds of questions, but you'll get a kick out of it.'"

Speaking of Corby...

If Arnold hadn't done his show solo, Corby Davidson may not have ascended to the heights he enjoys today at the station. When Arnold started his show, Mike Rhyner sat in with him for the first week to ease Arnold into the role of having to talk alone for two hours. But even after that week, Arnold still didn't feel comfortable. So, despite the protestations of then-program director The Laddy, Arnold took up on-air conversations with Davidson, who was his producer.

"I had a harder time than anybody else doing my show; if I was tired or not feeling well, there was nobody to carry it," Arnold said. "Everybody else had a co-host.

"Back then The Laddy didn't like the hosts talking to the producers or the board ops; those people were supposed to be invisible," he said. "It wasn't as freelance back then as it became. They were very structured; one host would take one side of an issue and the other host would take the other side. They'd debate it and the phones would ring.

"With me, it was just me," Arnold said. "I used to talk to Corby and it would drive The Laddy crazy. But I told him that Corby brings something to the table; they didn't realize back then how good Corby was. They just thought he was outrageous in the cubicle area, a hippie kind of a guy. But I spent hours with him off the air, whether it was formatting the show or just hanging out, and I realized he was quick-witted, clever and smart. I was going to use him on the air.

"Corby represented a demographic that might not call in—that just-out-of-college guy," he said. "I was going to bring the dynamic between he and I to the air."

But even though he had a guy to help bounce ideas off of on-air and help kill segments, Arnold was still feeling the strain of a schedule that was bursting at the seams. He was burning out quickly, but nobody realized it.

"Ya neva know" when it'll be time to go

Arnold was constantly struggling to juggle his multiple responsibilities. He loved his Ticket show, but he said it kept getting harder and harder to motivate himself to keep it at a high level. He was not only approaching the end of 1999, he was also approaching the decision to end the show.

"Remember, all the other shows had somebody else to pick up the slack if somebody wasn't feeling well," Arnold said. "I was giving it 100 percent all the time. My show was only two hours, but it was still two hours of talking about stuff. Plus, you always had to plan to two kinds of shows just in case a guest fell through.

"All these other guys would always plug who they were having on their show, but I never would," he said. "I know how these athletes and coaches are; you can't count on them. They say they'll do the show, but you don't know until they're actually on the phone or in the studio. So that's why I would always say, 'You never know who's going to be on that Ticket Hotline!'

"Plus, my show was more than sports stuff," he continued. "I'm really proud of the fact—and I tell Rhyner this—that I've got a whole lot of intellectual property that's still on The Ticket. It seems like every time I turn it on, either my name comes up or something

I did or started is being referred to, or there's an imitation of me, or they're playing an old sound byte.

"Like 'Movie Watching Is a Sport,'" he said. "This was crazy; I was already going to all these games, and Corby and I would go to review all these movies every week as well. I'd go on movie junkets to interview actors, all kinds of stuff. I had to maintain all of this and grow it.

"Add to that the constant adventure of just getting to the station every day, and that started taking a toll. Talk about wear and tear. . . . You have no idea."

Mavericks season was about to begin, and once again Arnold would be working a trifecta of gigs. And the pressure started making him think he was going crazy. He'd say things on the air that made no sense, like "This is Sportsradio 1310 The Ticket, I'm Chris Arnold and it's 10:35"—when it was 11:15.

"We would call it 'Chrislexia,'" Arnold said. "It would always happen on times or doing intros and outros. It would never happen during an interview or just talking to Corby. From day one, so I wouldn't get confused, I'd have my intros written down on a card. I would do an outro at the end of the *Dunham & Miller* show that went, 'The masters of mania, that sports juggernaut known as The Gentle Musers; ladies and gentlemen, the contagious hysteria offff...' I did that stuff each and every day, but I always had to have it written down.

"I did it so I wouldn't have to think about it," he said. "There was so much stuff going on in my mind all the time, it was wearing me out. I told Bruce Gilbert that August that I was burning out. He said, 'No you're not. You're all right.'"

Gilbert had good reason to try and dissuade Arnold from giving in to the feelings of "burnout" and giving up the show. After all, Arnold had proven a major success, repeatedly earning a No. 1 rating for his time slot in The Ticket's highly coveted demographic of men ages 25–54.

But it wasn't long before Arnold hit the wall. Just like that, one Friday after his show ended in November 1999, his time at The Ticket was over.

"I'm very competitive; I was burning out, and the last thing I was going to do was have a terrible show," Arnold said. "I wasn't going to be one of those guys who starts to have bad ratings and gets fired because he hung on too long. If I was going to leave, I was going to go out on top, on my own terms.

"There were some things going on that were building up in my mind; little things that shouldn't have bothered me were," he said. "Although the show sounded great, I felt I was losing my mind. I wasn't hard to work with, but I was tense. Nobody else saw it, and I didn't say anything about it, but the show was consuming me."

Part of the problem—other than exhaustion—was Arnold's perception that, after the firing of Chuck Cooperstein, he had become the de facto "sports guy."

"Chuck allowed the rest of us to venture away from being hardcore sports, because he covered our behinds," Arnold said. "He left and they brought in Rocco, who was, of course, a disaster. The listeners—not the other hosts, not station management, the listeners—would put pressure on me to be that hardcore sports guy. I was like, 'I'm not the *Higher Authority*; don't put that on me.'

"So one day I decided to turn in a letter of resignation," he said. "Nobody knew I was going to do it; they were in shock. It was effective immediately."

The shock was still prevalent the following Monday, when Bob and Dan took over Arnold's ten to noon slot and had no explanation for his absence. The conjecture started as to why he wasn't on The Ticket anymore, as is only natural when a host of a popular show leaves suddenly. He said a lot of people wondered why he didn't just quit K104 if he had to give something up. After all, he's a role player there, and he was a star at The Ticket. But his loyalty, and his bank account, wouldn't allow it.

"I'd been at K104 since 1980, and they let me cover just about everything there was to cover in the world of sports," Arnold said. "I knew I had to cut back on something, but the Mavericks were easy to do. That job wasn't wearing me down.

"Plus, K104 was the number one station in town, and The Ticket wasn't even in the Top 15," he said. "And K104 was paying me big money."

Arnold, who is still at K104 and helps emcee the Mavericks' in-game entertainment, looks back on his Ticket days with fondness.

"I enjoyed it immensely and developed great friendships," Arnold said. "I wouldn't have a family if it wasn't for The Ticket [he met his future wife, former Ticketchick Pamela, at a Guys' Night Out at the long-lost Bronco Bowl in 1998]. I wouldn't have traded it for the world. When people tell me they're still talking about me at The Ticket, I love it. It's nice to be remembered.

"The Ticket's a never-ending story, a soap opera. And the listeners are in on it. That's The Ticket's big secret: you're in on the deal."

Speaking of soap operas, here's the chapter you've been waiting for: The Ticket's most notorious ex-host, Greg Williams.

20

GREG WILLIAMS

The Hammer

FOR THE FIFTEEN YEARS The Ticket has been on the air, it's had its share of personality conflicts and guys who left under not the most pleasant of circumstances. But those things happen in any business; nothing had ever happened to shake the foundation of the station.

That all changed on October 12, 2007, when one of The Ticket's pillars, Greg Williams, abruptly left a remote held in Addison. It would be his final appearance on the station. The weeks that followed spawned heavy speculation of why Williams hadn't been heard from, most of it centering on rumors of drug use.

Turns out the rumors were well-founded.

Before going forward with the details of those weeks and the subsequent months, one thing has to be stated up front. No matter what listeners—or Williams' former co-workers—think of him, or how they think he may have screwed the station, nobody feels worse about what happened than Williams himself. He could have easily said "no comment" to the questions surrounding his departure, or not even bothered to respond to the message left on his phone. But he was more than straightforward in his answers, almost amazingly so. Take that for what it's worth.

And although he will always be remembered for the way he left the station, the time he spent helping make The Ticket into what it is today is also a story worth telling.

One hell of a bartender

Williams was born into a military family in 1960. And like most families of that type, his moved around almost constantly. Williams lived in Turkey and Spain, among other places, before his family finally settled in the Wise County city of Boyd, located thirty-five miles northwest of Fort Worth.

He lived there for six years until he left to attend Ranger Junior College on a baseball scholarship. He promptly flunked out.

"I flunked basically because I didn't have anybody there to make me wake up and go to class," Williams said.

For the next five years he worked as a bartender, a job that would serve him well when he became a radio host.

"Those five years were valuable to me because they helped me hone my people skills," Williams said. "You're dealing with drunks, so you have to have a little patience. The bars I worked at were the hottest ones in Fort Worth; on Wednesday nights we'd draw a thousand people. It helped me being in the public that much, being exposed to that amount of people every night."

He did his job well and says he made "a fortune" doing it. But it was a road leading nowhere, and he realized he had to make good on the promise he had made to himself to get a degree.

"My main job was chasing every single girl I could find and drinking as much beer as I could in the shortest amount of time," Williams said. "But a lot of people my age were already out of college and into their careers, and I sure didn't want to tend bar the rest of my life.

"I woke up one day and decided I was going to start applying to colleges, and within a couple of days I had applied to four of them," he said. "I always knew I was going to get a college degree. That was really important to me."

Williams eventually found his way to TCU, where he buckled down, grew up and graduated with a journalism degree in 1989. Channel 5 (KXAS) offered him an internship and he took it, starting down a path that would eventually make him a household name in the Metroplex.

The benefits of hard-ass work

During the internship, he said he "wormed" his way into the sports department and formed a friendship with sports photographer Kerry Smith, who let Williams work as his "grip" on the sidelines during football games. Smith showed him the proper protocol of being a member of the media, and he eventually helped Williams land a spot at WBAP.

"There are three people who were big-time instrumental in helping me: Kerry Smith, [WBAP sports director] Steve Lamb and Mike Rhyner," Williams said. "Kerry told Steve that I was a really hard worker who wanted to get into the business. Steve said he had a lot of work for me to do, but he couldn't pay me for any of it. And I didn't care."

Williams worked his way into a paid position at WBAP, first as a reporter and then as a producer for Randy Galloway's show. He covered countless sporting events but also covered the scene at Parkland Hospital on April 19, 1993 as casualties from the Branch Davidian conflict in Waco streamed north. Williams tried to wear as many hats as possible; he'd have cleaned the toilets with a toothbrush if they had asked him.

And on top of that, he was still bartending two nights a week.

"I'm living proof that if you work hard, good things can happen to you," he said.

Up on the roof

As discussed earlier, Williams knew Rhyner and Craig Miller from their days in the "back of the bus"—the auxiliary press box at old Arlington Stadium. One day in July 1993, Williams received a call from Miller that would ultimately change the course of his life.

"Junior called me and asked if I was going to the game that night, and I told him I didn't know," Williams said. "He said, 'You need to go, because Rhyner needs to talk to you about something. I can't tell you what it is.'

"So I went to the game that night, and Rhynes says, 'Let's take a walk,'" said Williams. "I'll never forget that. We stood on the top of the roof at Arlington Stadium and he ran the whole thing down: there was going to be an all-sports station, he was staffing it, and he wanted me, him and Junior to do a show together."

It sounded like too good of an idea to pass up, but Williams was hesitant. He had a job at WBAP that he loved, and he could see himself moving up. He thought he'd be there forever—he was just cocky enough to believe he'd outlast Galloway and take over his show. But the other side of his brain was telling him he'd immediately get to do his own show with Rhyner (and Miller, as was the plan before George Dunham entered the picture). Such an opportunity wouldn't exist at WBAP for several years.

He was batting the idea back and forth, and then WBAP made Williams' decision a lot easier.

"One night Kevin Brown was pitching for the Rangers. He threw a three-hitter but lost, 1–0," Williams said. "He broke every fluorescent light on the way to the clubhouse with a bat, and then tore that clubhouse apart. I'd known [Rangers first baseman] Rafael Palmeiro pretty well, and he said, 'Look at that attitude. That guy over there is killing us.'

"Reid Ryan, Nolan's son, was an intern at WBAP at the time; he had gone out on a few stories with me, so I had gotten to know him," he said. "He told me that night that his dad said Kevin Brown was the most selfish player he'd ever encountered in all his years in baseball."

Williams went on the air the next night doing the Rangers' postgame show (this was when WBAP carried Rangers broadcasts), and he went on a bit of a tirade about Brown. Without quoting either Palmeiro or Ryan, Williams asserted that Brown was one of the most selfish players in baseball and was killing the team.

Then he had to go to the principal's office.

"I got called in by the PD the next day and got read the riot act because the Rangers had complained," Williams said. "I said, 'Wait just a minute. People said this to me. I didn't attribute it to them because they trust me.' He said, 'You're not allowed to have opinions like that.' I said, 'What about Galloway and some of the stuff he says?' The PD said, 'Well, you're not Galloway.'

"I said it would never happen again, that I knew the rules and he wouldn't have to tell me twice," he said. "That was in September of 1993. I found the nearest phone, called Rhynes and said, 'I'm in.' There was no doubt anymore—I was looking for a sign as to what I should do, and that was it."

Time at The Ticket

Williams was obviously a huge Ticket presence, his "back porch witticisms" and redneck delivery earning him legions of fans. He, along with Rhyner, Miller and Dunham were The Ticket's Big Four from the start. But he wasn't exactly a polished broadcasting professional, and he needed a little help to get his Ticket career off the ground.

"I've got to give credit to Rhynes for that," Williams said. "He let me do my thing, and he protected me. I could give you a thousand definitions of that, but he just protected me. On second thought, 'protected' might not be the right word. He just kind of looked out for me, taught me how to be a talk-show host. He taught me how to act, when to get off the sports page and when to get back on it.

"We just learned how to keep people listening," he went on. "We learned who our audience was and how to keep them. It was as simple as that. We minimized the bullshit. A lot of people accused me and Rhyner of taking opposite sides of an argument on purpose, but that never once happened."

Not that they were big-time buddies off the air—at least in the later years. Starting around 2000, when the show ended each day, Rhyner, Williams and Corby Davidson would immediately disperse, barely saying a word to each other. "We always did that," Williams said. "We did our show, and when it was over it was like, 'See ya.' We were gone.

"We used to hang out before The Ticket when we were covering Rangers games, have a beer or two and get something to eat," he said. "But Rhynes had a family; he didn't have a lot of time for hanging out anymore."

The beginning of the end

If the end-of-show routine didn't indicate a cooling relationship between Williams and Rhyner, Williams' penchant for playing fast-

and-loose with the truth did. A seemingly innocuous lie Williams told regarding his sudden weight loss in 2004 planted, Williams said, seeds of distrust in Rhyner's mind.

"There was a problem between me and Rhynes," Williams said. "To this day I don't know exactly what it was; he just didn't trust me. I had that lap band surgery, lost a lot of weight, and lied to Rhyner about it because I was embarrassed. I never recovered from that."

"Our relationship was never the same," Rhyner said. "He said, 'I don't know what I've done to make you feel the way you obviously do, but I'm sorry.' I said, 'You don't know what you've done? Let me put it this way: do you have anything you'd like to tell me about?' I was giving him the chance to come clean, and he said no. I asked him again, and he said no again.

"Then I said, 'Let's go back to when you missed that time and you were in the hospital getting your gall bladder taken out,'" he continued. "'What did you really have done?' As I started down that road I saw the change in his face. He looked down, and without looking up he said he'd had the lap band surgery.

"That was when things really started to go bad," Rhyner said. "I don't know, maybe it had been cooling before that, but after that something happened. I realized then that I couldn't believe a thing this guy said. The way I saw it was, if he'd lie to me about something like that, he'd lie to me about anything."

But to the credit of both, they didn't let their growing animosity affect the show.

"We masked that pretty well on the air for a long time because we had a job to do," Williams said. "We were both pros. But it wasn't that bad then; it just got progressively worse. I think that I just wore on him. It's like a bad marriage; when a couple gets divorced after fifteen or twenty years and you ask them why, a lot of times they can't tell you. I think that's what happened; I wore on him and he couldn't trust me."

"It wasn't just me, though," Rhyner said. "He was a drain on everybody from about that point on. He was needy, needed so much attention. He would do or say just about anything to get it. Somewhere in there he completely and totally lost his ability to be one of the guys.

"He started doing something he used to rail on athletes for doing: loving the life more than the game," Rhyner added. "He loved the life more than his job."

Rhyner could barely tolerate Williams on the air and didn't want to be anywhere near him off the air. Williams later admitted to being addicted to a prescription painkiller, which he took to combat ongoing problems he was suffering from the surgery. Williams told Rhyner this the last day before the show went on hiatus for two weeks before Christmas of 2004, then he checked himself into a detox center for four days. At that point, Rhyner was very supportive of Williams. In fact, he'd had no idea his partner was going through the problems Williams was facing.

"I learned I was an addict," Williams said. "I convinced myself through withdrawals, cravings, pain, everything. It makes your skin feel like it's crawling off of you. I can still feel it."

As if enough wasn't already going down the crapper in his life, Williams was diagnosed with depression around that time. He was mysteriously absent for nearly three weeks in 2005, even missing *The Hardline*'s annual trip to Spring Training, an absence that was never explained on the air. By 2006 his on-air performances had deteriorated so badly that the management had several meetings with him regarding his repeated slurring of words. Williams would also, at times, utter nonsensical sentences and completely derail discussions by taking them in totally different directions from what was intended.

"It happened constantly," Rhyner said. "A lot of times it was because he was on something. But there were some other things that went on, too, like pouting fits, where he would sit in a corner and hardly say anything. It usually happened when he didn't think he was getting enough attention, or in pre-show meetings when we would want to do one thing and he'd want to do another. He wouldn't get his way and he'd pout.

"That bothered me more than anything. I told everybody that if

he kept doing that, I was going to tell him to go home. It never came to that, but I should have done it."

"I want to make it very, very clear that I'm not blaming depression or using it as an excuse for what happened," Williams said. "It's a condition I have, one I'm not running from or denying. It's not the reason things eventually went bad at the station.

The situation only worsened. Williams was slurring his words so badly at the Super Bowl in February 2007 that Bennett and Catlin later played the tapes for him to illustrate the problem.

"They asked if anything was wrong with me," he said. "I said no, that I was just taking this anti-depression medication. I guess they saw something was wrong with my performance and I didn't.

"That medication will change you," Williams said. "I have to take a handful of pills every day just to be normal. I'm the worst kind of depressant there is: I'm not quite bipolar, but I'm at the top of the manic depressive category. If I was bipolar, they could treat me with that kind of medication. If I was a little bit less depressed, I wouldn't have to take as many medications.

"It's hard to explain what it is. It's just a medical condition; 73 million people in this country are afflicted with it. With me there were days where it was all I could do to get out of bed."

It got so bad that Rhyner was seriously considering leaving the show himself if something wasn't done about Williams. "I'd pretty much made up my mind that once I got to the end of this contract [in February 2009] I was going to do something, and it wasn't going to include him," Rhyner said. "If that meant we stayed and he was gone, that would have been ideal for me. But if it didn't mean that, I was prepared to leave myself." He said he had talked to both Corby and Danny Balis about leaving with him—to whatever destination that might have been—if Williams didn't leave. There was talk of Williams leaving to do the morning show on sister station KPLX-FM, a country station. Nothing came of that, but both Rhyner and Williams knew the end was approaching.

D-Day

Whatever behind-the-scenes machinations were taking place regarding the show, it was clear that Williams was freaking out his co-workers; for one thing, he'd started collecting guns in late 2006. And their concerns aren't that hard to understand. After all, here was a guy who had been on so many drugs that he couldn't do his job effectively, with an arsenal of weapons he'd gladly show off to anyone who asked.

"It concerned me lots," Rhyner said. "He's very obsessive-compulsive; when he starts on something, he throws himself whole hog into it. And so it was with the gun thing.

"I told him, 'Look. You're a mental patient. Do you think it's a good idea for a mental patient to have all of those guns?' He said no, but he never did anything about it. He didn't think he had to answer to me. He didn't think it was my place to hold him accountable for anything.

"I think he owed me the same thing he owed everybody else up there—to do his job, and do his job well, stay within the confines of accepted behavior," Rhyner added. "He stopped doing all that stuff."

The guns, lies, anti-depression medication, painkiller addiction and his increasingly erratic on-air performances all slowly built up like a doomed house of cards. What happened October 12 at Blackfinn restaurant on Belt Line Road obliterated that house forever.

Williams had never missed a show meeting, was rarely even late, but on this day he didn't show up. Rhyner was pissed, but Corby was scared as hell.

"He was there, every day, for the eight years I worked with him," Davidson said. "I waited about fifteen minutes into the meeting and then I called him. No answer. I called his apartment. Still no answer.

"About two o' clock I'm getting ready for the show," Davidson continued. "I call him again, still no answer. We haven't told Dan Bennett, and Cat was out of town. Mike was like, 'Screw it.' Things weren't real rosy between them anyway.

"Two-thirty comes and there's still no word—from all I've ever known about Greggo, he's not the most stable of people," Davidson said. "I honestly thought he'd killed himself. I called Dan as I was driving to the remote and said, 'Look, I know Mike isn't going to call you, but I'm freaking out about this. I have a really bad feeling.' And Dan thought the same thing."

Bennett called Williams' apartment building and had someone go into his unit, but he wasn't there. This was about five minutes before Rhyner and Davidson were to go on the air to mix with *BaD Radio* in the "Why Today Doesn't Suck" segment. Davidson was relieved that Williams wasn't lying dead on the floor of his townhome, but he still didn't know what the hell was going on.

"We're about fifteen minutes into the segment with Bob and Dan—it's about 3:15—and all of a sudden Greggo calls [*BaD Radio* producer] Tom Gribble," Davidson said. "Greggo was talking from somebody's OnStar system in their car—at least, that's what he was telling us. I asked him, 'Dude, what the hell is going on?' He said, 'It's crazy, man. I'll tell you when I get there. It's just crazy.'

"He shows up right at 3:30 looking like shit," Davidson said. "What the fuck? He and Mike started screaming at each other, but I broke that up and asked him again what happened."

Again, Williams' penchant for lying bit him in the ass. Instead of simply saying he had overslept taking an afternoon nap—which he later claimed was what had happened—he concocted a story nobody came close to believing. He said he had been out on Lake Granbury, where he has a house, and his boat ran out of gas. He didn't have his car keys or his cell phone on him. He just happened to get lucky enough to drift to shore, he said, where he flagged down a passing car, hitched a ride from Granbury to Dallas, and called in on that car's OnStar system.

Stories don't get much more elaborate—or unbelievable.

"Yeah. He really expected us to believe that," Davidson said. "Mike called him a fucking liar. He got into it with Greg, and I got into it with him as well. About that time Cat called because Danny [*Hardline* producer Balis] had gotten a hold of him and told him what was going on. We're a minute away from going on the air and everybody in the bar can hear Mike and Greg arguing."

"I told him I didn't believe a word of the story," Rhyner said. "Then he starts talking to me about how I always walk around the station like I'm so self-important, and how I'm always trying to get people fired. He told me, 'You're not shit up there.' I was like, 'Where did all of this come from?' First of all, I've never gotten anybody fired, and I don't think about getting people fired. I don't roll that way.

"Whatever power I may or may not have up there isn't really that important to me," Rhyner said. "These days, I don't have that much anyway. Nobody does."

The argument between Rhyner and Williams continued to grow heated, to the point that a couple of listeners approached the table the hosts were sitting at, but immediately stopped in their tracks when they realized what was going on. However, once the theme song for the show started, all the hosts snapped into performance mode. They pulled off the first segment without a hitch.

"If you didn't know what had just happened, you wouldn't have known it by listening to us," Rhyner said. "I was really, really proud of us that day, and our ability to put all that aside and conduct ourselves professionally on the air. Little did I know that would be the last segment I'd do with the guy."

During the first commercial break, Jeff Catlin called Davidson and asked him to give the phone to Williams because he was going to ask him to take a drug test. "Greggo goes, 'Oh, Cat. Cat. Please. Why? Please. I gotta leave the show?' Davidson said. "Then he told us he had to take a drug test and I said, 'Well, go.' He put his head down and walked off."

And that, as they say, was that. Except for the fact that he failed to show up for the drug test, basically sealing his fate at The Ticket.

What does Williams now say happened that day? "I overslept. Simple as that. The Granbury story was a total lie, but that's what I told them. I don't remember Mike calling me a liar, but he'd have had every right to if he had.

"I was doing coke at the time and I had been doing it since May," he said. "Yes—that's absolutely true. I was doing my fair share; I wouldn't say 'hard,' but it was certainly more than every once in a while. But I don't think that played any role in being late. That was a one-time deal."

The coke was only a problem for a few months. But his performance behind the microphone had been an issue long before that.

"I had confronted him three times in the previous six months asking him if he was doing cocaine," Davidson said. "I've been around people who were into it before. He would show up to work with a nosebleed. He was really unreliable, really bad on the air. Really bad.

"Before that he [must have been] on something else, because he was slurring his words really bad," Davidson continued. "I told him they were getting ready to give him a drug test and that whatever the fuck he was doing, he better clean his ass up. But whatever he was doing, he stopped. After that he was just in another world. His job was to talk for four fucking hours and he couldn't put a sentence together. He was a fucking mess.

"If you're a hardcore listener to the show, [you know] that last year was a train wreck for him," Davidson added. "We had to treat him like a little baby. Some people caught on, some didn't. It was embarrassing. Our ratings were still good and it's a bottom-line industry. But when he skipped the drug test, that was it."

Still, even after blowing off the drug test, Williams thought he'd still have a job. This despite the incident at Blackfinn, despite the fact that he'd lied to several other Ticket hosts who suspected he was on coke and had confronted him about it. And despite the fact that his performance had gone down the toilet.

"I didn't take the test, but I didn't think my time at The Ticket was over," Williams said. "I didn't know what was going to happen; I just knew I'd have to be at the station at nine Monday morning to talk with Bennett and Catlin.

"They confronted me. There were never any voices raised, and I knew they had a legitimate concern," Williams said. "I told them, 'I didn't take the drug test because I can't pass it.' They told me I was doing the right thing by admitting it, and that they were going to get me the help I needed." Williams was told he wasn't going to be back on the air until management was convinced he could do his job again. He had to get totally clean, totally dried out, and only then would they even discuss putting him back behind a microphone.

November 2007 was the most hellish month of Williams' life. He entered rehab as an inpatient for five days, then an outpatient for the next few weeks. Every day, Monday through Friday, he had to show up for treatment from nine in the morning until four in the afternoon.

The pain medication addiction had just been detox—this was the real deal.

"Rehab was something that I put a lot into because I knew I had fucked up," Williams said. "I wanted to get better. I wanted to get back to work."

But he also wanted to kill himself.

On the brink

"The depression was hitting me really hard," Williams said. "I had the notes written and the gun in my hand." One of the letters was to Rhyner (he said he'd never divulge its contents), but this wasn't about losing a job at The Ticket.

"I remember I was so disgusted with myself, and I was hurting so bad mentally and physically, that I just didn't think I could go on," he said. "I don't know what pulled me back. I know this sounds squirrely, but I'm still searching for that answer.

"When I didn't do it, I felt even worse," Williams said. "Something wouldn't let me do it, but I was disgusted with myself that I couldn't go through with it. I thought I was a complete failure, a complete asshole. I was so low and disgusting I couldn't even kill myself. That's what I was thinking.

"But suicide is the most useless thing anybody can ever consider. I had to bury my brother; I can't believe that I ever got that far after seeing the pain my mother is *still* going through. If I put her through that again, that would be the most selfish thing I've ever done."

And all of this happened *before* the news that would shake him to the core.

Don't bother

Williams was nearly delusional in his belief he still had a place at The Ticket. Ostensibly cleaned up from the coke, he felt he'd be welcomed back, not necessarily with open arms, but welcomed back nonetheless.

Those fantasies should have been shattered for good the day before Thanksgiving, when a meeting that was meant to clear the air turned into open season on Williams. And he deserved every bit of it.

His Ticket career was over when he left that conference room.

"He looked good. He'd been in rehab for six weeks and gained some of his weight back; before that he was emaciated," Davidson said. "But he sounded like shit. All the hosts were there, as well as Danny, Dan and Cat. Danny said, 'The way you sound, we could not put you on the air today. You sound fucked up.'

"Everyone confronted him on every lie he had ever told them," Davidson continued. "He thought he was going to apologize, come back on the air the next day, and that would be that. But the last incident was the one that broke the camel's back. And there had been a hundred of them.

"When the product's starting to suffer because of one guy, you've got to get rid of him. They gave him a million chances, tried to help him a million times. And they got nothing in return."

For whatever it's worth, Williams sat through the barrage, Davidson said, without once arguing or raising his voice. He admitted he had lied repeatedly. He took the hits.

Williams saw the writing was on the wall, and it was obvious he was out. He wasn't fired, although someone else who was in the room said he quit three times during the meeting.

Merry Christmas, Hammer.

However crushed Williams may have been by the realization that he'd never again be associated with the station he loved, he realized he had no one to blame but himself.

"I thought I was bulletproof, I thought they couldn't do anything to me," Williams said. "And they proved me wrong."

Moving on

Life sans The Ticket has been largely uneventful for Williams, save for a cease-and-desist letter his lawyer sent to the station demanding that his drops not be used—and no disparaging remarks be aired about him—or else they would file a wrongful termination suit against The Ticket. So, for months afterward, Williams was referred to only as "He Who Must Not Be Named." Williams and the station eventually settled on a severance package in May.

For most of the summer, Williams was bored off his ass waiting to see if any other Dallas radio station would take a chance on him. He had a lot of time on his hands to think about where it all went wrong with The Ticket. He was basically bumming around—reading some, watching a lot of TV, trying to stay out of his girlfriend's hair. Williams finally received that second chance when ESPN Radio hired him to work the 7–10 P.M. shift.

"Anybody who says they'd be ecstatic if they won the lottery and didn't have to work—they're idiots," Williams said. "But when you screw yourself you have to take it, and that's what I did," he said. "I hated it; I really, really pissed away the greatest job in the world.

"But I did it. I did it. Nobody did it to me. Those guys did what they had to do. A lot of it I don't agree with, a lot I do agree with. And I think they'd be shocked with a lot of the stuff I agree with.

"There are things that I accept, and that I admit to," Williams said. "That I had a lot of trouble with the truth. My life was always easy; I was a master at taking the easy way out of everything. That's the first real hardship I ever had."

As clichéd and cheesy as it sounds, Williams said he once again likes the person who looks back at him in the mirror, as opposed to what he termed "the beast" that was peering back at him for most of 2007. His pain has abated, his anti-depression medication has been properly adjusted and he's got his girlfriend to keep a close watch on him.

"She pretty much lives with me," he said. "She doesn't let me get very far away; she doesn't trust me to take my medication or eat right. She was able to nurse me through the bad times. She probably saved my life."

Financially, he said, he could probably go until mid-2009 living the same lifestyle he became accustomed to when those fat Ticket checks were rolling in. He's got the lake house in Granbury and another home in Colorado. And he can't wait to sell the townhome on Turtle Creek where he spent the worst days of his life.

"I had to go to my Turtle Creek house today to get my mail. When I walk in there I get a chilling, eerie feeling," Williams said. "But when I get back to this lake house, I'm calm, collected, happy and content."

And he's still financially stable enough that he can buy a gun whenever he wants. Which is fine, just as long as he doesn't point one at his head again.

"I'm through that," Williams said. "I tried it once and couldn't do it. That only thing I shoot is a paper target at the gun range. I'd never kill anything."

Though his days at The Ticket are nothing but a memory, and he's basically lost touch with just about everybody at the station, he does have a message for Ticket listeners, staff and management.

"For the listeners: I'm sorry. And I really mean it. For the guys I worked with: no hard feelings. I don't know if they have them or not, but I know I don't."

From Rhyner's perspective, he said he may see a day when he and Williams can once again be friends. But it'll be a long time before that day comes.

"People don't believe it when I tell them this, but I'm not real good with grudges," Rhyner said. "I'm really a softie. As much as I may have the reputation for being a hard-ass, I'm really not. Time generally takes care of just about anything for me.

"I hope that maybe there will come a day when I think differently of him, but for now I'm still pissed off."

The sad departure of Greg Williams is in the past. To wrap up this book, we'll take a look at the station's future.

SECTION SEVEN

In for the Long Haul

21

THE FUTURE OF
THE LITTLE TICKET

THE TICKET has become so phenomenally successful in its first fifteen years, you'd understand it if George Dunham, Mike Rhyner or one of the other hosts mailed in a show every now and then. But they don't, because they retain the same hunger and drive to succeed that they've had since Day One. They realize how lucky they are to have fallen into the job of their dreams, and they never want to take their good fortune for granted.

"Everybody's much more confident in their performances, and more in tune with what the audience expects and wants," Dunham said. "There's nothing like having your own show fifty weeks a year for fifteen years. You know what's good, and you can go to that well on a consistent basis.

"It's a credit to the radio station and to the listeners that, for the most part, we can try just about everything," he continued. "If it works, great—they love it. If it doesn't work, then listeners let us know, and the guys are smart enough not to go back to it.

"We've always had this bond with listeners—we're regular guys who are sports fans, just lucky enough to work here. Listeners feel they're a part of the station, and the guys feel the same way. These are our listeners—we know them. They can't be duplicated and they can't be underestimated."

But while the bond between The Ticket and its listeners has been incredibly strong since 1994, how long can it last? By the fifteen-year mark, most radio stations have already changed format two, three or even more times—what can The Ticket do to maintain the momentum it's enjoyed for an almost ridiculous amount of time?

The two men who were intimately involved with building the station into what it is today—and the two men most responsible for guiding it into the future—have some definitive opinions about what the station will look like when its twentieth, twenty-fifth and thirtieth anniversaries roll around.

Voices from the past looking to the future

The Laddy and Bruce Gilbert deserve most of the credit for helping The Ticket find its legs and reach unexpected heights, respectively. Both keep tabs on the station as best they can to this day, and both have a good idea of what it will take to keep it a success.

"I would hope that the station can continue to look for new, fresh and exciting things to do," said The Laddy, "to find new and talented individuals while holding on to their core group of guys. They all have such great work ethics, I could see them all staying for at least another ten years.

"I've always got my eye on that station, because I still feel connected with all those guys," he went on. "What's unique about them is they have a shit-pot of money, and that's usually when the work ethic of on-air talent—the thing that makes all of them keep doing the things that got them there—starts to backslide. And they haven't started to backslide yet.

"This is usually the time in the lifespan of a station where, during contract negotiations, they'll start to go, 'I don't have to do this,' or 'I don't have to be at Ticketstocks,' or 'I don't have to call in to the other shows anymore.' But these guys realize they found each other at the right place and at the right time. Their hard work is what got them to where they are."

At some point, obviously, it'll come time for all the hosts to leave. For some there will be age concerns. Others will get tired of the hours, still others will feel it's time to pursue other interests. And when that time comes, it'll be up to a new generation of Ticket torchbearers to keep the brand going strong.

"It'll be difficult, and they might take a hit; they might have to take a step back before they re-tool," The Laddy said. "You have to constantly reinvent. It's interesting; at some point, like anything, it will change. It's a question of how well they can keep the spirit of the station. There won't be another Rhyner, of course, but you can find a different twist on things.

"If I were running that station during the next generation, I'd buy a house and make the future stars—the ones who work nights and weekends now—I'd make them live with each other, like a *Big Brother* or a *Survivor* sort of thing. Make them hang out and see if there's a bond between them. That's what the original Ticket guys had, and that's hard to find."

Gilbert said The Ticket will face the dual challenges of integrating new talent and trying to figure out how to remain relevant in a medium that becomes more and more of a relic as new technologies continue to seep into the entertainment and communications industries.

"I'm glad it's not my issue," Gilbert said. "The station, as I've said before, has a certain personality, with people who can relate to all of the traits that exist within that personality. [The guys at The Ticket] probably are running the risk of not feeding the 'young end' of that personality, if you will.

"And I don't just mean that from a demographic perspective, not so much from a figurative sense as a literal sense," he said.

"The world is changing; the difficulty The Ticket faces is the same that every radio station faces: How do we exist [once] we've been tagged—and we really can't deny it—as an old medium in a world with all these new technologies?

"The Ticket needs to re-create some of that bunker mentality, not necessarily in terms of the on-air talent but in terms of other platforms, such as an alternative channel on the Web. I'd be looking at new technology as a way to develop and ingrain new talent that can be the guys of the future for that radio station."

That's obviously much easier said than done, but Gilbert said he's confident the stewards of the station's future, program director Jeff Catlin and general manager Dan Bennett, have a good plan. It's definitely a tough problem to tackle, however. Gilbert brought up the example of The Eagle (KEGL-FM), which used to be hands-down the dominant rock station in Dallas. It was, in fact, the envy of rock stations across the country. But it ran out of gas, becoming a mere shell of its former self. That, Gilbert said, is a fate The Ticket must fight hard to avoid.

"I'm not trying to forecast the death of The Ticket," Gilbert said. "To the credit of Dan Bennett, Jeff Catlin and everyone else there, they have lasted far longer than anybody could have imagined. That's a remarkable feat they should be proud of."

The fight to last

Catlin and Bennett are obviously well aware of what faces them as they steer The Ticket toward more milestone anniversaries. While Catlin is focused on the technologies the station might employ to continue to thrive, he's just as intent on making sure the talent well remains stocked.

"I think about it every day," Catlin said. "That's my job. I'm not doing my job if I'm not prepared for every eventuality.

"All of our guys are hugely successful; they all want to be here," he continued. "We have a great team. They all will be here as long as they want to be and as long as we can keep them here. But it's my job to look for talent, develop talent, and have a Plan A, Plan B and Plan C. I've even got to find somebody to take my own job if I leave.

"Every day I'm thinking about who's next and what's next, and what we're going to do today to maintain our position," Catlin said. "The people across the street want what we have, and I'm not going to let them get it. And everybody here feels the exact same way. If we don't keep our eye on the ball every day and seriously come in here and bust ass just as hard as the day before, there's always somebody behind us ready to take it.

"Where the guys push themselves in the future will be by understanding when it's time to jettison the old, boring crap and bring in things that are new and off-the-cuff that turn into something great."

But while the "old guys" are still on board, it's critical to get as much out of them as possible. That's why Catlin, Bennett and others at the station are exploring ways to exploit new methods of digital media, such as an enhanced Internet presence, podcasting, streaming audio and possibly even satellite broadcasting of some sort.

"I don't know where everything is going, but we're about content, entertainment and personalities," Catlin said. "We need to make these guys available in as many ways as possible so people can develop a relationship with our guys, our station and our brand—wherever that may be.

"I'd also like to be, for lack of a better term, the station of record in Dallas-Fort Worth—like KMOX in St. Louis, WGN in Chicago or KOA in Denver," he said. "Whatever that station is that means 'community,' that's what I want The Ticket to be.

"Not to be cocky or anything, but to a certain extent, for guys anyway, even if they're not super hardcore sports fans, I think they like listening to The Ticket," Catlin said. "They're aware of it, and they want to get The Ticket's take on the big subjects. It's almost like it's not real until the guys at The Ticket get the chance to talk

about it. I think The Ticket really developed that during 9/11; that's where we really took a turn and showed another side and grew, helped develop a bond with the community.

"We always have to change and give our audience something new while remaining true to who we are."

Evolve or perish

Bennett echoes the sentiment of keeping a vigilant eye out for new talent while making sure the presentation in its current form remains fresh.

"I tell Jeff a lot that one of the mistakes you make is when you're winning and you say, 'Don't touch anything. Let's just ride it out,'" Bennett said. "That's the wrong strategy. If you're green you'll grow—if you're ripe you'll rot. Once you think you're where you need to be, people become complacent.

"The Ticket has a philosophy of 'Keep making left turns,'" he went on. "If we did the same promotions year after year the same way, our audience would get bored with us. That's why the guys on the air, who are brilliantly talented, have to keep re-inventing themselves every day, every week, every month, every year. They have to."

The definition of "re-invent," in Bennett's terms, goes farther than Gordon Keith introducing new, fresh characters to the morning show. It also means finding new events with which to showcase The Ticket. Charity Challenge on Ice ran its course, so they created a flag football game. When that ran its course, they played a baseball game at Dr Pepper Ballpark in Frisco. What's next, a basketball game? (Let's hope not.)

"It's got to be different, have a twist," said Bennett of future Ticket events. "An example is Ticketstock. We change the floor plan and look of the stage every year, because, again, our audience will get bored if we don't.

"It's like a pro sports team," he said. "If you run the same plays, you become predictable. And when you get predictable, you get beat. .

"The station is going to continue to evolve," Bennett said. "The station has made personalities out of everybody associated with it. The on-air talent is obvious, but we've made household names out of Big Strong [Jeremy Moran] and Grubes [Michael Gruber]. We have to continue to add new characters and people to keep it interesting."

"We have to continue to develop new and upcoming people. Gordon Keith used to just be a guy who drove The Ticket Hummer. Corby used to produce Chris Arnold's show. Donovan Lewis was a board op for KLIF. Talent can be an engineer, a board op, a sales guy or a caller. We have to bring that new talent in so the station can continue to grow."

Not only does The Ticket have to continue re-invent for its own sake, it also has to evolve in order to keep the competition at bay. While most casual observers scoff at any other local sports station becoming a threat, Bennett maintains a healthy respect for ESPN Radio, and any other sports station that may emerge in the future.

"We always respect our competitors, and we need to stay focused on what we do," Bennett said. "We're still the number one station, but we conceded a long time ago that not everybody likes our shtick. There are people who like hardcore sports, and there's an outlet for that.

"But Mike Rhyner had a great line awhile back that went, 'We can do what they do, but they can't do what we do,'" he said. "We can switch gears at any time and do hardcore sports better than anybody. But when I hear our competitor try and do shtick, I don't think they're in the same league.

"This station isn't built around any one person; it's built around a team of brilliant people. I heard Jerry Jones say once that you can't have enough stars. That's how we're going to do it: evolve, grow and add more stars."

The last word comes from The Laddy himself, sage words that should serve as "locker room" material, of sorts, for every Ticket employee, now and in the future:

"The fundamental things to remember are these: provide a product that's entertaining, informative, credible and unpredictable," The Laddy said. "Have a bunch of guys who go above and beyond the call of duty, and make the listener believe this is some sort of fraternity that he wants to be a part of. And never, ever get to the point where the hosts feel they're doing the listeners a favor by doing a show for them.

"If The Ticket does all of that, it will remain successful."

CHURCH.

— ACKNOWLEDGMENTS —

WRITING MY FIRST BOOK was the hardest thing I've ever tried to do. I knew it would be hard, and a whole lot of work, but it's also been the most satisfying project I've ever completed.

And there are a lot of people I have to thank for their support and encouragement, starting with my wife Kelley, my mother Allene, my father Bryan, my aunt Iris Tillis, my brother Andy, my father-in-law Richard Moon, my mother-in-law Diane Moon and all of my other friends and family members.

I especially want to thank Jeff Catlin, Dan Bennett and every other member of Ticket management who made this book possible. The access they provided was unbelievable; they showed enough faith and trust in me to let me do what I needed to put this together.

Most of all, though, I want to thank every single Ticket host, all the former hosts who have moved on, and every behind-the-scenes person. They were all incredibly gracious with their time and open with their stories.

And, of course, I want to thank every P1 who picks up this book. Without your dedication to The Ticket, the station wouldn't be worth writing a book about. Hopefully you've learned something about this incredible radio station. I'm honored to have had the chance to write its story.

ABOUT THE AUTHOR

SCOTT BOYTER is a bonafide P1 from Day One and editor of *The Sports Page Weekly*, a Dallas sports newspaper. The Dallas native graduated from the University of North Texas in 1993—about four years longer than it should have taken him—with a bachelor's degree in journalism. He lives in Dallas with his wife Kelley and their four cats.